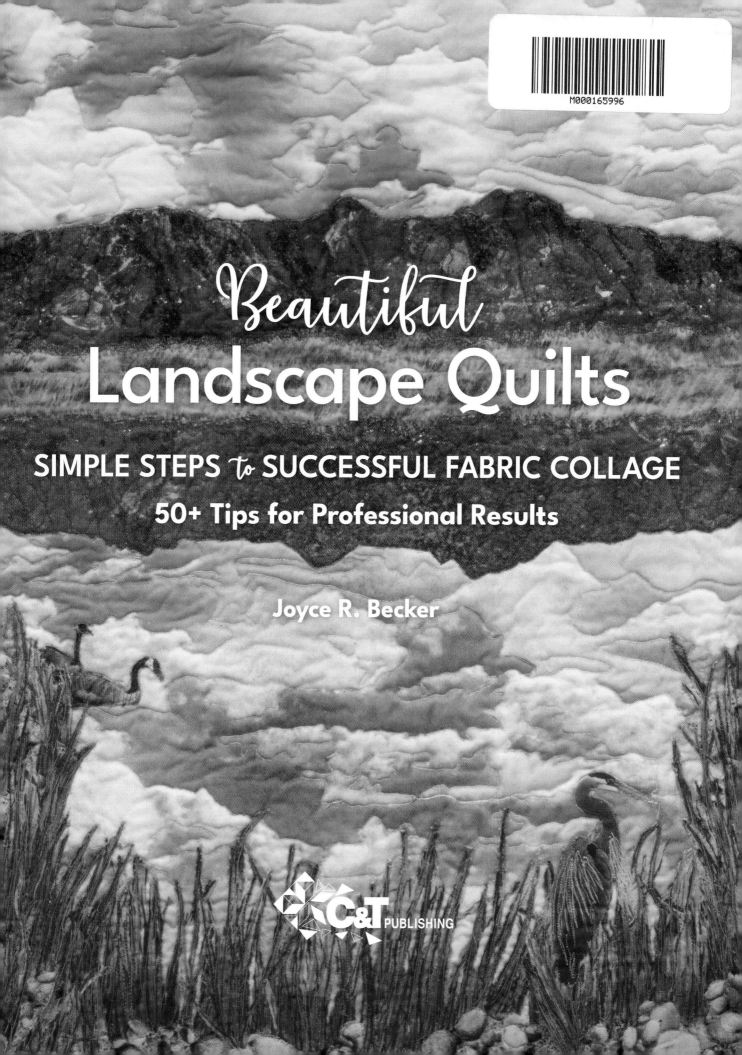

# *Beautiful* Landscape Quilts

## SIMPLE STEPS *to* SUCCESSFUL FABRIC COLLAGE

### 50+ Tips for Professional Results

Joyce R. Becker

C&T PUBLISHING

Text and photography copyright © 2022 by Joyce R. Becker

Photography and artwork copyright © 2022 by C&T Publishing, Inc.

Publisher: Amy Barrett-Daffin

Creative Director: Gailen Runge

Acquisitions Editor: Roxane Cerda

Managing Editor: Liz Aneloski

Editor: Kathryn Patterson

Technical Editor: Debbie Rodgers

Cover/Book Designer: April Mostek

Production Coordinator: Zinnia Heinzmann

Production Editor: Alice Mace Nakanishi

Illustrator: Linda Johnson

Photo Assistant: Gabriel Martinez

Front cover photography by Lauren Herberg of C&T Publishing, Inc.

Instructional photography by Michael R. Simmons; subjects photography by Lauren Herberg of C&T Publishing, Inc., unless otherwise noted

Published by C&T Publishing, Inc., P.O. Box 1456, Lafayette, CA 94549

Library of Congress Cataloging-in-Publication Data

Names: Becker, Joyce R., author.

Title: Beautiful landscape quilts : simple steps to successful fabric collage 50+ tips for professional results / Joyce R. Becker.

Description: Lafayette, CA : C&T Publishing, [2022] | Summary: "A complete guide to designing and making landscape quilts, from inspiration to final display. Step-by-step instructions and photos. Guest landscape quilt artists include Heidi Proffetty, Annette Kennedy, Nanette S. Zeller, Lenore Crawford, Cindy Walter, and Helene Knott"-- Provided by publisher.

Identifiers: LCCN 2021036970 | ISBN 9781644031223 (trade paperback) | ISBN 9781644031230 (ebook)

Subjects: LCSH: Quilting--Patterns. | Landscapes in art.

Classification: LCC TT835 .B33165 2022 | DDC 746.46/041--dc23

LC record available at https://lccn.loc.gov/2021036970

Printed in the USA

10 9 8 7 6 5 4 3 2 1

## Dedication

I dedicate this book to my stepson, Mike Simmons, and his lovely wife, Charlene. They traveled all the way from Colorado to photograph the instructional shots in this book and assist me with the planning, layouts, photography, and computer issues. Thank you from the bottom of my heart.

## Acknowledgments

I would like to thank the entire team at C&T Publishing. It has been an interesting period of time working together using a Google Drive to create this book. I specifically want to thank all of you for having the patience with me to learn how to navigate the new technological challenges.

In particular, I would like to thank the following C&T staff: To managing editor Liz Aneloski, thank you for leading me through every step of the way. To acquisitions editor Roxane Cerda, you have been such an incredible resource for me. To Amy Barrett-Daffin for continuing to be the best quilting book publisher in the industry, and to Gailen Runge, Todd Hensley, Kathryn Patterson, Debbie Rodgers, April Mostek, Zinnia Heinzmann, Alice Mace Nakanishi, Linda Johnson, Estefany Gonzalez, and Gabriel Martinez—thank you for your continued support and assistance writing this book.

I would also like to extend a heartfelt thank you to each of the talented contributing landscape quilt artists featured in this book: Lenore Crawford, Annette Kennedy, Helene Knott, Heidi Proffetty, Cindy Walter, and Nanette S. Zeller. I feel blessed that you accepted my invitation to be included and furnished me the information necessary to write your profiles. I am thrilled to be able to showcase your inspiring landscape quilts.

A very special thank you to my dear friend Jan Nield for adding borders and quilting *Swept Away* for me.

To my amazing husband, Donald, who continually supports me and realizes that creating words and landscape quilts are my passions.

# Contents

# Introduction

Although I have written several quilting books on the subject of landscape quilting, my goal in this book is to include more instructional photographs that actually show you techniques versus just telling you about them. If you are like me, I learn much easier when I can actually see something visually instead of reading instructions. My hope is that this book will enlighten you and equip you with the tools and knowledge that you need to create successful landscape quilts.

I am thrilled with the opportunity to include several talented and famous landscape quilt artists in this book, giving you the opportunity to witness their incredible art and learn what makes their art unique. Hopefully you will be excited to see how they create their quilts and learn about their techniques. I cannot thank them enough for letting us view their spectacular work and learn about them.

There are so many new methods and technologies that we can incorporate into our art quilts that were not available to us in the past. For example, you will find a lot of information on how to incorporate digital images into your art in this book. Also, the fabrics available today are making a huge impact on landscape quilting. From digital fabric panels that are incredibly realistic to ombré fabrics that automatically build in perspective in our landscape quilts, not to mention nature-themed fabrics, we artists are very fortunate because designing is so much easier with the right fabrics. I am also including a whole chapter in the book with lovely photographs of some of the fabrics that I recommend and use.

One of the highlights of this book is to help you achieve realism in landscape quilts. Whether you use landscape fabrics, digital images, or create your designs using coloring mediums or by combining any or all of these choices, I hope this book will provide the knowledge you need to blossom, to try new options, to put fear aside, and to just have fun with your art. As I have always said, "There is no failure when you try something new. If something doesn't work, just try another pathway and eventually you will have success." I once had a brand-new quilting student in a workshop at the International Quilt Festival in Houston, Texas, who said, "Joyce, I will never be able to create a landscape quilt." I believe one reason she succeeded is because she knew nothing about the "quilt police" and she just let her imagination guide her. I was blown away because she created the best design in the workshop. So, never give up; my methods make it easy for you to create a successful landscape quilt.

Writing this introduction actually brings tears to my eyes. In a particularly unusual time in history, I found solace writing this book and creating quilts. The discipline I've had for getting up each day with goals to accomplish gave me a creative mission. It is my fondest wish that each of you finds joy in creating quilts. Be proud of your accomplishments, listen to that voice in your head that says, "I love my quilt," and find joy because you have succeeded.

# Quilting Tools and Supplies

## Rotary Equipment

When creating landscape quilts, you will need a rotary cutter, cutting mat, and a quilting ruler. Here is an example of a kit that comes with all three components. I suggest purchasing a rotary cutter that comes with 45mm blades.

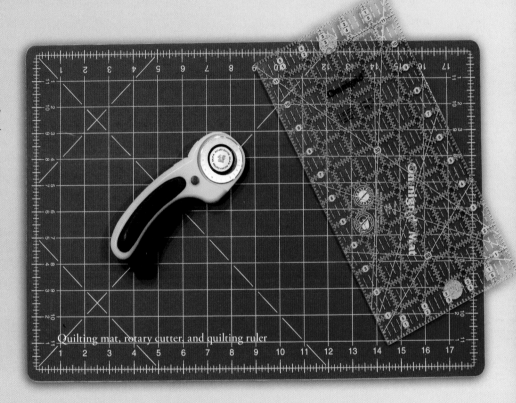

Quilting mat, rotary cutter, and quilting ruler

Karen Kay Buckley's Perfect Scissors—4″ Green and 6″ Blue

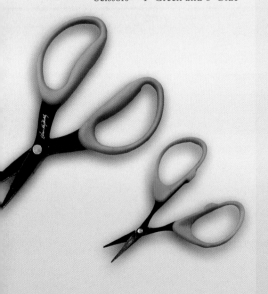

## Scissors and Tweezers

Sharp scissors are an absolute necessity for realistic cutting when creating landscape quilts. There are two types of Karen Kay Buckley's Perfect Scissors that I recommend. The small green scissors are 4″ with microserrated blades, and they are terrific for cutting smaller elements in nature, such as leaves, flowers, or trees. The larger blue scissors are 6″, and they are best for cutting larger slices of fabric.

One of the contributing artists in this book, Heidi Proffetty, has designed an amazing pair of Precision Tweezers for quilters. You can use them in many ways, but they are perfect for picking up small pieces of fabric that have been cut and glued, ready for placement in your quilt design.

Heidi Proffetty's Precision Tweezers

www.heidiproffetty.com

Chapter One: Quilting Tools and Supplies    7

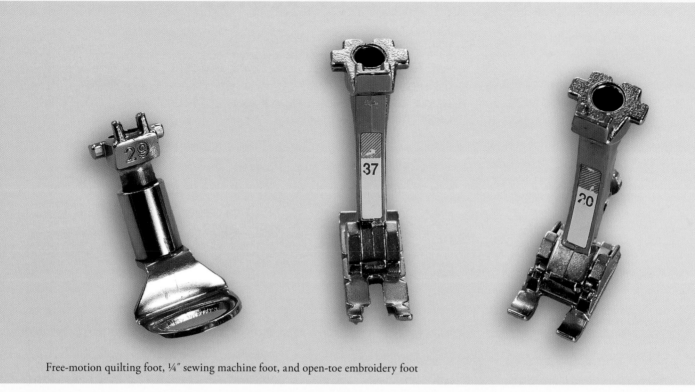

Free-motion quilting foot, ¼″ sewing machine foot, and open-toe embroidery foot

## Sewing Machine and Accessories

A sewing machine with the ability to lower the feed dogs for free-motion work, with an accompanying plexiglass extension table, is important in making landscape quilts.

You will need a sewing machine foot specifically for free-motion work including basting, free-motion embroidery, and quilting. There are many options available depending on your brand of sewing machine. I recommend a large closed-toe round foot. You will also need a ¼″ foot for sewing on the binding or facing on your quilt. You may need an open-toe embroidery foot too.

## Repositionable Spray Adhesive

You will need a repositionable spray adhesive to temporarily position fabrics on the canvas as you build your design. There are many brands of spray adhesive that indicate that they are repositionable, however, 505 Temporary Adhesive for Fabric (by Odif) is worth the investment. The other adhesives do not successfully hold the elements onto your canvas as long as the 505 spray. If you are allergic to spray adhesive you can use a glue stick or Roxanne Glue-Baste-It, but your fabric pieces won't be repositionable.

# Irons and Starch

Any fabrics that you will be cutting into need to be starched *heavily*. Starching the fabrics heavily gives you more control when you are cutting. I prefer mixing Purex Sta-Flo Liquid Starch with water and placing it in a spray bottle. My mixing formula is two-thirds starch and one-third water, shaken well. Spray both sides of the fabric and give it a few minutes to soak in so the iron doesn't stick to it. The fabric should practically stand up by itself after using this method.

*Tip* Always put the starched fabric with the wrong side up on the ironing board when pressing with a traditional iron or a heat-press, otherwise, you might end up with a glossy or shiny surface on the front. Consider starching your fabrics in the kitchen sink for easy clean-up.

Any kind of regular iron that doesn't leak is fine for this type of quilting and you will need a regular-size ironing board. The smaller Oliso iron is perfect for pressing bindings and facings on your quilts and works really well with a wool pressing mat. If you plan on making landscape quilts in the future, it might be worth it for you to invest in a heat-press. The heat-press without steam works best for ironing large quantities of starched fabrics. Remember to put the wrong side of the fabric up when ironing.

*Tip* I typically use an old iron for starching my fabrics. It doesn't matter if it gets dirty; I just clean it and use it again and again.

*Tip* It is not necessary to starch the fabrics that you won't be cutting into, such as sky fabrics. You only need to press the wrinkles out of these fabrics with steam.

Liquid starch and spray bottle

Regular iron and Oliso iron with wool mat for pressing

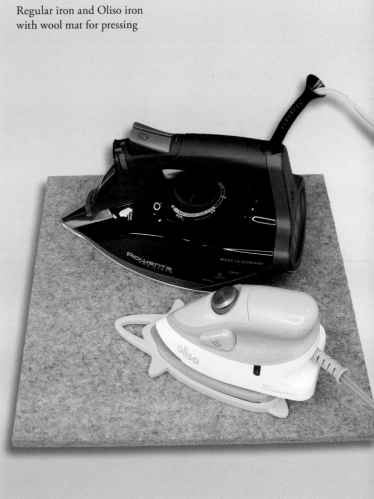

# Threads and Needles

## Thread for Basting

Instead of a transparent thread that stretches, is thick, and breaks easily, the thread I am recommending is revolutionary. I recommend the 60-weight Madeira Monofil Clear thread and I only wish I had discovered it years ago. This thread is so lightweight you can hardly see it and it sews like butter. For most quilts, I suggest basting your quilt with the clear thread but for really dark quilts, use the smoke color. I typically use the Monofil thread in the top of the machine when I baste quilts and use an InvisaFil (by WonderFil Specialty Threads) matching bobbin thread in the bobbin. Monofil can be used in the bobbin when you are quilting if you don't want your quilting to show.

## Free-Motion Embroidery Thread

For the free motion raw-edge embroidery phase of stitching when the quilt is a top, you can use a variety of threads that either match or enhance the portion of the design you are working on. Chapter Seven (page 55) delves into raw-edge machine embroidery and thread choices.

## Bobbin Thread

For free-motion embroidery bobbin thread, use a matching lightweight thread. InvisaFil is my bobbin thread of choice first because it is 100-weight and hardly shows, and second because it is available in 60 different colors. It can also be used for hand appliqué.

When I am machine quilting, I typically use a matching InvisaFil thread in the bobbin. Chapter Seven (page 57) talks more about bobbin thread recommendations.

Assortment of InvisaFil bobbin thread
(by WonderFil Specialty Threads)

## Quilting Thread

As with your free-motion embroidery, you want your quilting thread to match or enhance the elements *on the top* of your landscape quilt. Since most of the intense portion of your thread work is done during the free-motion machine embroidery stage, all you need to do is quilt on top of the free-motion machine embroidery but not as heavily or as densely. Use the same threads you used in the free-motion machine embroidery stage. It is, however, important to quilt with the same density throughout the quilt so it will hang nicely. (For more information on quilting, see Quilting, page 63.)

## Sewing Machine Needles

**FOR BASTING:** Match your needle to your thread. If you are using 60-weight Madeira Monofil thread, use a microtex #60 needle.

*Tip* Microtex needles are not as sturdy as some but they don't leave large holes in your fabric. When you stop and start your stitching, turn the handwheel on your machine gently versus pushing on your foot pedal, otherwise the needle may break.

**FOR FREE-MOTION MACHINE EMBROIDERY:** If you're using a 40-weight or lower thread, use a jeans/denim #70 needle (it helps with skipped stitches).

**FOR METALLIC THREAD:** Use a metallic #80 needle (it helps prevent shredding).

**NOTE:** If none of the above work or your thread is too thick, try a topstitch #90 needle or an embroidery #90 needle.

## Batting

Because landscape quilts are meant to hang on the wall as art, it is important that you do not use a high-loft batting. Your goal is to have your art hang as flat and nice as possible and Hobbs Thermore batting will accomplish that goal. Other options are Hobbs wool batting or a cotton batting.

*Chapter Two*

# Getting Started

## Design Inspiration

Design inspirations are everywhere in nature. Learning to look at nature with a new set of eyes, noticing things you've never noticed before, may help you when you try to decide what your landscape project will be. For example, when you see a forest you automatically think, "Well, duh, it's green." Indeed, it is, but how many shades or values of green do you see?

Is the sunlight creating a lighter value on some of the leaves or boughs on the trees or are some of them in shadow? What shapes are the elements that you see? For example, try to visualize how a cluster of leaves looks on a tree as pictured in the stand of quaking aspen trees in the next photo. This photo was taken on the Last Dollar Road, which runs through the heart of the Rocky Mountains just outside of Ridgeway, Colorado. Can you see all the textures, the shadows, and markings on the trees?

What I am trying to articulate is for you to try to notice all the little things in nature. If you use the same green fabric for the entire forest in a design, your quilt will be pretty boring or unremarkable. What you want to strive for in your designs is to have a strong *visual impact*. That doesn't mean the values and colors of your fabrics have to be bold, loud, or colorful, in fact the mood of a landscape can be soft and comforting, but the choices you have made to make it appear realistic and interesting are what is most important.

Last Dollar Road, Ridgeway, Colorado
Photo by Michael R. Simmons

## Landscape Moods

I strongly believe that landscape quilts *can* exude moods. For example, when I created my quilt *Aloha Spirit*, I was dealing with some overwhelming chaos in my life. I needed something to calm me down, some place where I could take a quiet walk on a beautiful beach with sparkling water and colorful palm trees blowing in the wind. So, since I couldn't be there in person, I created the environment or the *mood* of peaceful waters lapping onto the shoreline in the tropics.

*Aloha Spirit by Joyce R. Becker*

## Where to Find Landscape Inspiration

So, where do you find an inspiration for your landscape quilt? There are many ways to discover landscape design inspirations.

1. Like me, you might see a design or a visual inspiration in your mind.

2. Perhaps you have traveled somewhere and captured inspiring photographs that can be your design inspiration.

3. Maybe you have a post card or a greeting card that inspires you.

4. How about photos you have taken in a beautiful garden?

5. You may have browsed through a beautiful coffee table book or photo book full of inspirational photographs.

6. What about a place or time when you made a special memory? Could that be an inspiration for your design?

*Tip* **Please realize that you cannot copy someone else's art without their written permission. As much as you would like to create their art using fabrics, understand that you *could* be sued for copyright libel if you do so. What you can do, however, is contact the artist for written permission to recreate their image as a landscape quilt. I've contacted many artists during my career for permission to use their art as an inspiration for a quilt. A large majority of the artists were thrilled and gave me written permission to do so.**

If you are considering recreating a work of art from a famous artist who has passed away, the copyright statutes vary according to where and when the art was created. Sometimes, the family of the artist who created such a work owns the copyright even if the art was created a hundred years ago.

## Beginning the Design Process

Now that you have decided what you want to create, let me help you begin the process.

1. If you are using a photograph, enlarge it to 8½″ × 11″ and print a color copy. Now print another copy in grayscale, which will help you with value decisions later on in your design.

2. If you don't have a photo and you have just an idea, do a rough sketch with a sky, midground, and foreground on an 8½″ × 11″ piece of paper. You can make it a vertical landscape or a horizontal landscape depending on your vision.

3. Think about how you can *simplify* your design. You don't need to include every leaf, every blade of grass, or every tree, rock, or stone. Leaving negative space (translated, areas like sky or water) is important for your design so that the eye moves across the entire scene. If your design is too busy, there is no relief, and you won't know where to look.

4. Just because you have a photo, you don't have to copy it exactly. You make the choices. Maybe you want more sky or not as much foreground or no foreground at all. I give you permission to alter your photographic image to suit your needs.

## Creating a Stabilized Canvas

In order to create a landscape quilt, you need a base to build your design on. I start with a piece of bleached or unbleached muslin stabilized with Pellon 906F Fusible Sheerweight interfacing or Pellon 911FF Fusible Featherweight interfacing. Since the interfacing is only 20″ wide, you may need to butt up or overlap the interfacing on your muslin canvas. You don't have to use the most expensive brand of muslin, just make sure it is wide enough for your design.

### Choosing a Size

First, you need to decide if your landscape quilt is going to be vertical or horizontal. If this is your first design, start with a reasonable-size quilt. A starting point might be 20″ wide and 24″ long, or 24″ wide and 20″ long. Allow for design shrinking due to the quilting, threadwork, and trimming, so start with muslin at least 4″ larger in each direction, so 24″ × 28″ if designing a 20″ × 24″ landscape. Purchase at least ¾ yard of a medium-weight bleached or unbleached muslin that is at least 40″ wide and purchase 1½ yards of 20″-wide sheer or featherweight interfacing to create a design using these dimensions.

How large you make your landscape quilt depends upon how big you want your quilt to be *without* borders. It is necessary to add approximately 2″ to each side of your canvas to compensate for shrinkage when you add machine embroidery and quilting, and you square your quilt later on. If your muslin canvas isn't wide or long enough, you can butt up another piece to extend the width or length. You can do the same with the interfacing. Don't, however, use a dark or printed fabric for your canvas because dark or printed fabrics will compete and cause shadowing with the fabrics in your design.

### Why Do I Need Interfacing?

Your next question is probably, "Do I really need an interfacing?" I learned *why* an interfacing is really a crucial component to the design the hard way. If you have no interfacing when you are basting or accomplishing the free-motion machine embroidery on your quilt top, the quilt top will sink down into the thread plate hole and get stuck. Having the interfacing also allows your design to remain smooth versus having an uneven surface, especially since you will incorporate different fabric weights.

### Steps to Create a Canvas

**1.** Use a rotary cutter and a cutting mat to cut the muslin and interfacing the same size.

**2.** Do your best to make sure the top and the bottom of the muslin canvas is level; it helps during the entire designing process.

**3.** Press all the wrinkles out of the muslin using steam because you don't want a lumpy, bumpy canvas. It will ultimately show through to your design.

**4.** Adhere or fuse the interfacing to the muslin using the manufacturer's instructions.

*Tip* Place a nonstick appliqué pressing sheet on your ironing board. Put the muslin facedown on top of the pressing sheet after it has been pressed, and then put the bumpy side of the interfacing facedown on the muslin with the smooth side of the interfacing up, and press. Fusing it this way will result in a smooth surface. Use a medium heat setting with steam. If the interfacing bubbles, your iron is too hot; if it doesn't adhere, the iron is too cool.

## A Working Wall

If you are not familiar with what a working wall is, it is a specific place where you can place your canvas to begin the designing process. One of the most important elements when designing a landscape quilt is to build in the correct perspective which we will explore in Scale, Perspective, and Value (page 27). When you place your project on a working wall you are able to stand back and see if everything is coming together as you expect it to. You can tell if your perspective is accurate and if you have used the correct values of fabric. You will also be able to tell if the scale or sizes of the fabric elements are acceptable.

For my working wall, my husband bolted office dividers made of a foamy material into the wall of my studio and we originally covered them with batting. Recently, we removed the batting and covered it with a white flannel sheet which is easier to pin into.

 **Many quilters are finding that covering their working walls with a white flannel sheet works better than batting because you can remove the sheet and wash it when it needs to be laundered.**

My working wall with an inspirational drawing divided into thirds, a stabilized muslin canvas divided into thirds, and the resulting quilt, *The Smoky Mountains*

Position your working wall somewhere that you can stand back and look at your design from a distance. If you try to design a landscape quilt flat on a table, it is difficult to build in the correct perspective. There are those quilters who don't believe this is necessary but trust me when I say, "*Please design your quilt on a working wall.*" It's also a vitally important place to audition fabrics and to check values. Using a working wall is just as important for other types of quilting too. For example, you can arrange traditional quilting blocks on your design wall to configure them. You can check to see if the values in your quilt work together and you can also audition border and binding fabrics.

Here are some recommendations for creating a sturdy design wall:

**1.** Measure the wall dimensions where you will place your working wall.

**2.** Go to your local hardware or building materials store with your measurements.

**3.** Go to the construction area of the store and look for an insulation board.

**4.** Insulation board comes in many thicknesses. Try to find one that is between 2″ and 4″ thick. If you need to use two boards to fill a larger space in your studio, they can be taped together with duct tape. You can also ask an employee to cut the boards smaller for you if necessary.

**5.** Use the silver side for the front of the working wall design board because the markings on the back of the design board will show or shadow through the batting or flannel sheet that covers the design board.

**6.** You will need a flat white flannel sheet or batting to cover the design board. Measure the size of your working wall to determine how large the sheet or batting needs to be and add 4″ all around so you can wrap the sheet or batting around to the back of the insulation board and staple it into place.

**7.** Although your working wall can just lean against the wall in your studio, I recommend actually screwing it or bolting it into the wall.

**8.** Place your canvas on your working wall, making sure the canvas is level. You are now ready to begin the design process.

*Tip* If you have any extra insulation board, don't throw it away. You can use it for a portable working wall when you travel for a workshop. Just cover it with batting.

*Tip* If you are unable to actually create an insulation board working wall, you also have the option of taping batting or flannel to an empty space, such as a closet door, as a temporary working wall. Tape the top, sides, and bottom with blue painter's tape so the working wall doesn't lift if a window or door is opened.

## How I Store Fabric

Before I delve into the types of fabrics available for us today, I would like to show you a photo of how I store my fabrics. Using an Ikea storage system, I separate my fabrics by elements or themes. For example, I put all my "tree" fabrics in one bin, my "mountain" fabrics in another bin, my "sky" or "water" fabrics in another bin, and so on. My storage system is away from the window and the harsh sunlight.

How I store my fabrics

## To Wash or Not to Wash

I am often asked, "Should I wash my fabrics before I include them in a landscape quilt?" Your quilt will be displayed on the wall and won't be used on a bed so there is no need to launder the fabric or the quilt itself. If your quilt gets dusty, take it outside and shake it, or place a layer of tulle over it and vacuum it gently with an upholstery brush.

 **You may want to consider spraying your quilt with a UV spray for textiles if it is in direct sun light, so it won't fade.**

## Types of Fabric

We are very fortunate with the wide variety of fabrics available to us today. This hasn't always been the case and in the past, we landscape quilt artists had to search far and wide for suitable fabrics or create them ourselves. We can go online and order hand-dyed or hand-painted fabrics or guess what … we can create them ourselves. Commercial cotton prints featuring elements suitable for landscape quilts are widely available and surprisingly realistic. The digital prints featuring landscape panels offered today are very representative of what we actually see in nature. We also have the capacity to take photographs ourselves and upload them into the computer and print them on fabric using inkjet printers.

### Hand-Dyed or Painted Fabric

Hand-dyed and hand-painted fabrics are a wonderful addition to a landscape quilt, especially in elements like sky and water. Both of these types of fabrics are available commercially but why not try your hand at creating them yourself? You can follow my instructions on how I painted the background fabrics for the water, sky, and sand in my quilt *Aloha Spirit* (page 83) and create your own.

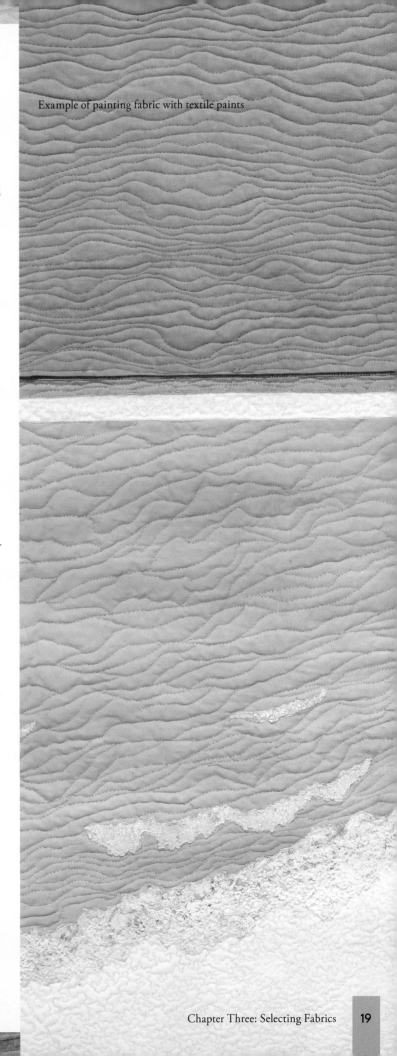

Example of painting fabric with textile paints

## Using Textile Paints

Typically, transparent textile paint is a better option than opaque textile paint unless you are painting dark elements. Opaque paints cover dark areas whereas transparent textile paint lets more light shine through. When you use textile paint on fabric, most manufacturers suggest you use a one hundred percent cotton or silk fabric with a tight weave. Although it is a bit more expensive, painting on cotton sateen fabrics with transparent textile paint versus painting on white muslin or even a PFD (prepared-for-dyeing) fabric is remarkable. The wonderful sheen of the fabric actually shows through even after it is painted. There are many varieties of textile paints and fabrics available at quilt shops, craft stores, and fabric stores. I list some of my favorite online shops in Supplies and Resources (page 124). Specific project quilts in this book will provide more details on how to paint fabrics.

A good resource for hand-painted fabrics with landscape themes is Mickey Lawler's Skydyes Fabrics (see Supplies and Resources, page 124). Hand-dyed fabrics are readily available both in quilting shops and online. Check your local quilt shop to see what hand-dyed or hand-painted fabrics they offer or take a look online at equilter.com.

## *Batiks*

Cotton batik fabrics are truly a joy to work with, especially as background fillers. I use batik fabrics in almost every quilt I make. Almost any quilt shop you go to will have a line of colorful batik fabrics. Generally speaking, batik fabrics are tightly woven cotton and they come in a large number of varieties. Hoffman Fabrics and Northcott Fabrics have lovely lines of batik fabrics.

Assortment of batik fabrics

## *Commercial Cotton Prints*

It is such a joy these days to be able to go into a quilt shop and find a variety of commercial prints to include in landscape quilts. From rocks to trees and bushes, leaves to grasses, and so on, more quilt shops and online sites are supplying us with everything we need. Here is a sampling of the Naturescapes collection by Deborah Edwards for Northcott Fabrics. This line is one of my favorite resources for realistic commercial landscape fabrics.

A selection of hand-dyed and hand-painted fabrics

*Naturescapes collection by Deborah Edwards for Northcott Fabrics*

*Fabrics from Stonehenge Gradations Ombré collection by Linda Ludovico for Northcott Fabrics*

Northcott also has a wonderful fabric line suitable for landscape quilts titled Stonehenge Gradations Ombré, designed by Linda Ludovico. The fabric itself ranges in value from light to dark and has many valuable uses. For example, if you want to create ranges of mountains using a gray ombré gradation piece of fabric, you can use the lightest value in the fabric as the mountains the furthest in the distance and then increase the value as you add more rows of mountains. It is an incredibly easy way to create perspective in designs without having to purchase multiple fabrics. For example, in my quilt, *The Smoky Mountains* (page 94), I used two different colorways for the mountains, starting with light values and moving on to medium values and then the darkest values.

There is also a line of Stonehenge Gradations fabrics that are wonderful for a large variety of landscape quilts. Here is a selection of samples from that line.

*Fabrics from Stonehenge Gradations collection by Linda Ludovico for Northcott Fabrics*

Fabric and pattern designer and C&T author Jennifer Sampou also has designed ombré fabrics in her Sky collection that are truly magical and beautiful. The fabric is just perfect for sky and water.

*Sky collection ombré fabric by Jennifer Sampou for Robert Kaufman Fabrics*

## Digital Prints and Images

With the digital age, we are very fortunate to have the availability of digital prints and images to use in our quilts. Many of these prints come in a panel format and the realism is remarkable. My suggestion is to shop for digital prints that you like and combine them with other appropriate fabrics in your stash to create a realistic landscape quilt. It isn't necessary to include the whole digital panel in your quilt, but it certainly makes designing much easier. My quilt *Majestic Mountains* (page 67) actually includes portions of two separate digital prints as well as other commercial prints. Instructions to create this quilt are in Chapter Eight (page 67). Keep in mind that specific panels I mention may not continue to be produced by the manufacturer. I suggest going to your local quilt shop first. If you come up empty handed, try searching online for "digital quilting fabric panels, mountains" and so on. For my favorite spots to find digital panels, see Supplies and Resources (page 124).

Detail of *Majestic Mountains* (full quilt, page 67) incorporating two digital prints

Here are two examples of beautiful digital prints provided by Timeless Treasures Fabrics (see Supplies and Resources, page 124) that could be used in landscape designs.

*Digital landscape prints by Timeless Treasures Fabrics*

Northcott Fabrics also has some wonderful digital panels to incorporate into land-scape quilts. The Swept Away collection is one of my absolute favorites and includes coordinating fabrics for borders and backing. My friend Jan Nield added borders to the panel and quilted it for me.

P&B Textiles (see Supplies and Resources, page 124) is another great resource for realistic digital panels to incorporate into your designs.

*Digital panels from P&B Textiles*

Swept Away, *panel by designed by Deborah Edwards and Melanie Samra for Northcott Fabrics, constructed and quilted by Jan Nield, 43" × 49", 2020*

## Printing Photographs on Fabric

Sometimes it's fun to create fabrics yourself using photographs that you have taken. In my quilt *Precious Moments with Blondie* (page 72), I actually incorporated several photographs I took myself and enlarged and printed the images onto computer-ready cotton fabric.

Detail of printing on fabric in *Precious Moments with Blondie* (full quilt, page 72)

## Online Printing

Sometimes you or someone you know takes an amazing digital photograph that just begs to be printed on fabric larger than a traditional 8½″ × 11″ image that can be printed at home. The wonderful thing about sending your image away online to be printed is that it can be enlarged and printed on a specific type of fabric that you select. One of my favorite images features Mt. Rainier photographed by Dan Neil. Here is the original image printed on organic cotton sateen at Spoonflower (see Supplies and Resources, page 124). You can see the finished version enhanced by quilting and other embellishments in Chapter Eight, *Mt. Rainier* (page 79).

Original photograph of Mt. Rainier

Photo by Dan Neil

## Chapter Four
# Creating Your Design

Except for a college class in art history, I have no art background. You don't need to have an art degree or an art background to create landscape quilts. However, if you are looking for help when it comes to selecting a palette of colors for your landscape design, I say go to the experts. Katie Fowler has designed an innovative Foolproof Color Wheel Set (by C&T Publishing) that includes die-cut discs and a printed color wheel to help you with ten different color configurations.

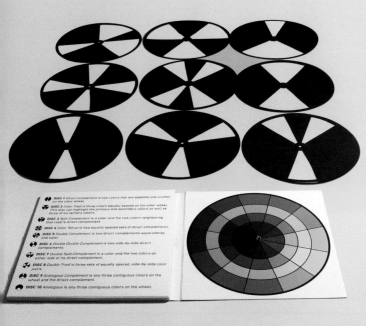

Foolproof Color Wheel Set by Katie Fowler

Now it's time to begin creating your design. You might be saying, "But Joyce, I don't know what fabrics to buy or how much fabric or what goes with what, I am so confused." There are no rules when it comes to creating your design with different fabrics. Whether the fabrics are commercial prints, solids, cottons, silks, dyed, or hand-painted, what matters most is if the fabrics "play nicely together". When you begin a new design, you need to look at your photo, sketch, or inspiration and decide if you want the colors and the values to be the same as in your inspiration or if you want to change your color palette. The "quilt police" won't come after you if you decide to alter your inspiration and play with the colors, using Katie's Color Wheel, or if you change the values, scale, or the mood of the design.

Next, you need to start pulling fabrics from your stash that you think will work. If you don't have a stash then it's time for a shopping trip to your local quilt shop or a shopping trip on the internet. If your local quilt shop doesn't have the fabrics you need, try equilter.com. Click on cotton prints and then check out the fabrics that are in different categories, such as forests, water, and so on. You can also check out the latest digital prints as a category. Chapter Three (page 18) shows you a large variety of fabrics suitable for landscape quilts so keep those in mind as you do your shopping.

# Auditioning Fabrics

When I talk about fabrics playing nicely together what I want you to do is lay the fabrics that you intend on using in your design together. Do any of the fabrics say, "Yikes, I don't belong with these other fabrics?" Sometimes, it will be necessary to delete one of your favorite fabrics, other times you may discover that the value of a fabric will be too strong and just overtakes the others or, just the opposite; you might have a fabric that blends in too much. You have to trust your judgment and just go for it. Frankly, there have been times when I think a fabric is perfect when I purchase it but when I put it on my canvas on my working wall with the other fabrics that I am auditioning, it just says, "I am way too busy, or the value is all wrong, or what was I thinking when I bought this?" With time, your eye and your mind will begin to tell you what fabrics work together and what fabrics don't work together.

On the left are clear colors, and on the right are muddy colors

A good rule of thumb when you are starting out and creating a palette of fabrics is to put "clear" colored fabrics together and put "muddy" colors together and *try not to mix the two*. There are those fabrics that are borderline that can go into either category, and it is fine to use those. Just use your intuition and ask yourself, "Do these fabrics look good together?" If your fabrics don't work or blend together your project won't be successful.

## *Background Fabrics*

Believe it or not, when selecting fabrics for your design, *the most important fabrics are the background fabrics*. If the sky or water fabrics don't enhance your design, your landscape quilt will never jell or look right; that's why auditioning your fabrics together is so important before you actually begin. Generally speaking, you can incorporate many types of fabrics for your backgrounds. Once you start designing your quilt and building your design from the top down, if the sky fabric distracts rather than enhances the design, now is the time to select another fabric. It is easier to substitute fabrics when you are in the design stage versus after you baste it and proceed with the construction.

 *Tip* Sometimes, the only thing that is wrong with a fabric is that the value is too strong. Think about using the wrong side of the fabric and/or putting an overlay over it.

# Scale, Perspective, and Value

Keep in mind that when you build your design, the elements in your scene will be smaller in the distance and as you come forward in your design, the elements will increase in size or scale.

The value of the fabrics used in your design also plays an important part in creating the corrective perspective. A tree in the distance, for example, should be lighter in value than a tree in the foreground. In fabric lingo, value just means your fabric is categorized light, medium, or dark. There are times, of course, when a scene you are creating might be in the shade or it might be a nighttime scene. The same rules apply for the scale and perspective of the design, but the values will be different.

Specific details in the elements in your design will be more prominent in the foreground of your design versus further back in your design. For example, you might be able to see the veins in a leaf on a tree in the foreground whereas you won't notice those details in the midground or distance in your scene. You create the correct perspective in your design when you incorporate realistic values and scale.

Example of light, medium, and dark values of fabrics

## *Modifying Fabric Values*

So, what if you find the perfect fabric but the value is too strong? Easy peasy, just think about putting an overlay of a lighter value tulle or organza over that portion of your design. Another option is to use the wrong side of a fabric if the value is too strong. Or, what if you have some beautiful flowers in the foreground of your design and you have the perfect commercial print, but you dislike the colors or values of the flowers? There are many ways you can recolor the flowers to make them perfect. I'll share with you how to do these techniques a bit later but just remember it is a possibility. The following example shows a scene with a mountain in the distance. The value of the mountain is too strong because your eye goes right to the mountain and doesn't flow over the whole design. The second image shows the mountain with an overlay of organza over it, correcting the value.

Mountain without overlay

Mountain with overlay of organza to lighten the value

# Rule of Thirds

When you design a new project, try to visualize it into thirds, for example, sky, midground, and foreground. The thirds don't have to be equal. Maybe you are doing a scene in Montana where the sky is larger than a third. What matters is that you have an actual placement guide for where your fabrics should go on your canvas. Here's how to accomplish the rule of thirds in your quilt design:

**1.** If your design inspiration is a sketch you have drawn horizontally, or it is an enlarged photo on an 8½″ × 11″ piece of paper, fold your paper or your photo horizontally into three equal parts, regardless of where the sky, midground, and foreground are on your inspiration.

**2.** Follow the Steps to Create a Canvas (page 15) for your design. Fold the canvas into thirds as you did with your inspiration.

**3.** In the margin of the canvas, place small pencil marks to indicate where the folds are.

**4.** Pin your design inspiration on your working wall right next to your marked canvas.

**5.** Check your design inspiration to see how far the sky extends into the design. Do you need less fabric or more fabric than where the first line or fold is? This placement guide tells you approximately how much fabric to cut.

**6.** If your design is horizontal, for example, and is 42″ wide, cut a 42″-wide piece of fabric and eyeball how far down your fabric needs to extend by checking the fold lines on the photograph or sketch.

# Cutting Fabrics

Generally speaking, you should try and cut the elements in your design as you go. Remember, most of your fabrics need to be heavily starched before you cut into them. Using my cutting techniques in conjunction with the heavily starched fabrics will give you realistic shapes. For example, when you design from the top down, the first thing you will cut is the sky. Use your rotary equipment to ensure the top line of the sky is level. If your design has rows of mountains after the sky, you will cut the starched mountain fabrics next.

*Tip* **It is not necessary to starch the fabrics that you don't cut into to create a shape or an element, such as the sky or water. All you need to do is press all the wrinkles out of these fabrics.**

If just "eyeballing" your fabric and cutting a row of mountains does not work for you, here is another option:

**1.** Measure how wide your mountains are; that's how wide you will cut your fabric.

**2.** Take a look at your inspiration placement guide and canvas to see how much fabric you think you will need.

**3.** Cut a piece of starched fabric approximately an inch wider than what you need.

**4.** Place your fabric right side up on a table and looking at your design inspiration; use a pencil to draw a row of mountains directly onto the fabric trying to emulate what you are seeing. Remember, the mountains furthest back in the design should be the lightest and, in most cases, the smallest.

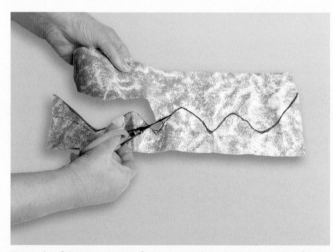

Example of drawing a row of mountains directly onto starched fabric and then cutting

*Tip* **Use the same fabric for two rows of mountains. Use the wrong side of the fabric for the mountains that are the furthest back. Your rows of fabric don't have to be the same color; it's the value that counts. Unfortunately, this trick doesn't work for batik fabrics as they have no wrong sides.**

## Move the Fabric When You Cut

Now it's time to cut the actual mountains. Cut just below the drawn line on the fabric. If you control the fabric with your left hand and cut with your right hand, moving the fabric, not the scissors, you will get much more control. You may want to try this technique on a scrap piece of starched fabric first. *Don't move the scissors*, move the fabric with your left hand. Once you get the hang of it, you will realize you have more control, especially when you are trying to cut small, detailed pieces of fabric.

## Realistic Cutting

Since we are talking about cutting, let's discuss the importance of cutting some of the elements you include in your design a bit more in detail. When I created *Precious Moments with Blondie* (page 72), I included a large grassy area just beyond the fenced garden. It's simple to just take a piece of commercial fabric and add it to your design but it may not look natural. I still crave the realism that detailed cutting provides and I hope you will too. Again, starch is really your friend, especially when trying to create small realistic elements. Here is a photo of how I cut the grasses that extended over the edges of the river in the aforementioned quilt.

Example of realistic cutting of detail elements

# Building the Design

Always build your design from the top down; that's the easiest and most efficient way to create your design. As I mentioned earlier, try your best to keep the top edge of your first fabric, in most cases the sky, level with the top of your canvas.

## *Focal Points*

Some landscape designs have focal points and others don't. So, what do you think happens if you put your focal point dead center? Your eye will always go to the focal point in the center and not across the entire surface of the design. Here's a suggestion; if your focal point is a mountain, don't put it in the center, put it on either side of the center and try and balance it with a focal point in the foreground on the other side of the design. In my quilt *Mt. Rainier Reflecting in Tipsoo Lake* (page 88), for example, the mountain is not dead center. The flowers and grasses on the bottom right of the quilt become the second focal point. The scale of the second focal point does not need to be as large as the basic focal point.

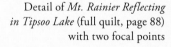

Detail of *Mt. Rainier Reflecting in Tipsoo Lake* (full quilt, page 88) with two focal points

On the other hand, my quilt *A Winter's Night* has no focal point. Sometimes a quilt is just a lovely vista with no focal points.

Your design needs to be balanced so none of the features overtake the other features or elements. Think about the actual scene or the inspiration you selected for your design. Whether you selected your inspiration for a specific reason, because of a mood, an emotion, or a memory, or just because it is somewhere that is beautiful doesn't matter. Your job is to make your design realistic and balanced.

**A Winter's Night** *with no focal point*

## Gluing

**1.** If you are using a spray adhesive (see Repositionable Spray Adhesive, page 8) for gluing, you need to have proper ventilation. Open a window, open the door to your studio, and turn on a fan or a ceiling fan when you spray.

**2.** Find a flat box to lay your fabric in to spray the back with glue. A flat cardboard box that has about a 1″–2″ lip works really well. Lay your fabric to be glued face-down with the wrong side up.

Box for spraying

**3.** Spray the back of your fabric liberally. If you don't spray enough glue onto the elements, they will fall off your canvas.

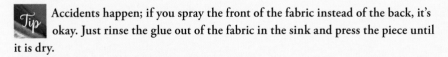 **Accidents happen; if you spray the front of the fabric instead of the back, it's okay. Just rinse the glue out of the fabric in the sink and press the piece until it is dry.**

**4.** Sometimes it is easiest to go ahead and glue and position the background fabrics into your design first. For example, position the sky first and if there is water in the foreground, go ahead and glue and position it into place too. This will help you position the rest of elements in the design.

**5.** Gently lift up your glued fabric and position it onto your canvas. If you have a lump or bump, just pick up the edge of the fabric and reposition it. If you don't like the placement, lift up the whole piece of fabric and reposition it.

**6.** If one of your fabrics isn't working, it is easiest to remove it now and try a different fabric.

**7.** After your background fabrics are positioned into place, ask yourself, are the fabric values correct, that is lighter in the distance and darker in the foreground? This is the time to think about an overlay of tulle to change the value of a fabric if necessary or even selecting a different fabric. Try auditioning several values of tulle in different colors to get the exact effect that you want.

**8.** After you select the tulle, cut a piece a bit larger than the area you will put the overlay on. Give the tulle a very light spray of the adhesive and position it into place. Later on, when you baste the design, you will stitch the tulle into place and cut away the excess.

Two layers of a tulle overlay on the dark green fabric in *The Smoky Mountains* (full quilt, page 94); cutting away excess after gluing and basting around the edges

**9.** Now it's time to add the other elements in your design. Start adding elements from the top down in the distance remembering to consider the scale or size and the value of the fabrics. Continue until your entire design is glued into place.

**10.** Stand back from your design wall and look at your landscape. Do the scale, the values, and the perspective look correct? If not, now is the time to make changes.

 **Remember, the spray adhesive is repositionable so you can move elements around or replace them if necessary.**

## Editing

Editing your design is crucial. It is easy to put too much "stuff" in your design so it looks cluttered. If your eye stops on an object when you look across the surface of your design, perhaps it doesn't belong in the design or the value or scale is wrong.

My quilt *Nightglow in Hawaii* (page 105) includes a large variety of trees, ferns, and other vegetation and it is quite busy. In order for everything to meld together and be similar in value, I placed an overlay of dark navy tulle over the entire quilt except for the sky.

## Photograph Your Design

Now, here is the final test. Take a photograph of your quilt top on your working wall and then take a look at the photograph. Sometimes, you will think your quilt design is perfect until you look at the photograph. A photograph will tell you what's right or what's wrong. Don't be disappointed if you have to make changes because the end result will make you much happier.

### Note: Machine Basics ∽

*When you create landscape quilts there are a few things you need to keep in mind regarding the upkeep of your sewing machine. First, always use a new needle for every project. On some projects, you will use different sewing machine needles for different processes. Keep your machine clean and oiled. When you work with raw-edge machine embroidery, you generate a lot of fuzz and dust from the fabric. When your machine starts to misbehave or sounds funny or clunky, it is an indication that you need to remove the throat plate, pop out the bobbin and the bobbin spool, and clean it out. I use a small paintbrush to clean my machine and I do it quite often. Please don't use the compressed air that comes in a can; it can damage your machine.*

Detail of *Night Glow in Hawaii* (full quilt, page 105) with a dark blue overlay

# Basting

When you are happy with your design and all your elements are layered and glued into place, now is the time to baste it. Don't get scared, this doesn't mean you have to hand stitch everything down; you will be using your sewing machine. Basting means you are going to hold all the layers of the fabrics in place by stitching free-motion around each of the element's edges with the monofilament thread I mentioned earlier and a matching bobbin thread. We do this step so none of the fabrics move or fall off of the canvas during the rest of the construction process. Here's what you need to do:

1. Lower the feed dogs on your sewing machine.

2. Put a free-motion foot on your sewing machine.

3. Use a new needle, preferably a microtex #60 needle.

4. Thread your machine with 60-weight monofilament thread and a matching 100-weight bobbin thread in the bobbin.

5. Use a piece of like fabric to test out the tensions in your machine.

 **I often adjust my top tension to zero when stitching free-motion.**

6. Adjust the bobbin tension in your machine if necessary. You want the thread to spool out at an even pace with just a little bit of drag on it.

7. Once the tensions on your machine are adjusted, place a sample with some of the same fabrics under your presser foot for a final test to see if the tension is correct. When the tension is correct, place your design under the presser foot.

8. Make sure to pull the bobbin thread to the top before you start stitching and stitch in needle-down position.

9. I always suggest stitching down the most precarious or smallest pieces of fabric first.

10. Take a few stitches in place when you begin, trim off your threads, and then begin stitching around the elements.

11. It is permissible to travel from one area to another because your thread is invisible.

12. You don't have to stop and start, trimming your threads each time.

13. Go around the outside perimeter of each element. No worries if you travel off the edge; just get back on track and keep going.

14. When you travel between elements use a curvy stitch instead of a straight line because the eye always goes to a straight line versus a curvy one.

15. If the edges of some of your elements become unglued during the process, don't worry. A bamboo skewer used for barbecuing is a good tool to slide under the needle to hold an element down while you stitch it. The skewer normally won't break.

 **Do not use a regular stiletto to hold down the elements while you are basting. You risk breaking your needle and the stiletto and having an eye injury.**

How to hold elements down during the basting process

## Chapter Five

# Cutting Edge Techniques

Every day it seems like a new idea or thought pops into my head when I think about how I want to create a landscape quilt. Whether it is a new technique or seeing a vision of something in my head that I want to try, I normally just go for it. Not all of my trial-and-error experiments work out but what happens in the process is that it may lead me in another direction. I am not afraid to try new stuff; if I fail, I fail and then I'll try something else. That's what I am trying to encourage you to do. Failure actually leads to creativity if you open your mind to the concept.

## Incorporating Digital Images

I know that discussing the many options of incorporating digital images into your landscape quilts might be new to you but later on in the book, Chapter Eight (page 67) demonstrates examples of quilts made with digital images. Once you see how easy it is to incorporate digital imagery, I hope you will give it a try.

### Printing at Home

There are many times that I have taken photos of elements in nature and actually printed portions of the photos to include in my quilts. For example, in *Precious Moments with Blondie* (page 72) I took photos in my garden and incorporated some of the printed images I did at home on my all-in-one HP inkjet printer. The specific elements I incorporated were hosta and hydrangea plants and flowers. I typically purchase whatever brand of *white* sew-in colorfast fabric sheets for inkjet printers that are available at my local quilt shop or fabric store. Unfortunately, these fabric sheets are *only* intended for inkjet printers, not laser printers or printers that use heat.

Once you decide you want to incorporate part or all of a photo into a quilt, you will need to upload the digital photo into a photo software program. Several free programs on the internet work well if you don't have a photo program on your computer. Both Gimp and Fotor are easy to navigate, even for beginners. Always save your original photo in case you need to refer to it later. After your photo is uploaded, you simply crop the photo to include only the areas that you want to print. Next, print the copied image on regular copy paper in grayscale to see if it is the size you want and make adjustments to the size as needed. You can make other adjustments, such as using a filter to improve the sharpness of your photograph or changing the hue and saturation to improve the colors, so experiment in your photo program and don't be afraid! Once you have the correct size, save it as a new file and print it in color on a fabric sheet.

Print your photograph on computer-ready fabric in "Best" mode to get the highest-quality print that you can. I recommend taking your photographs using a high-resolution or "pro" mode on your smartphone or a digital camera when you photograph in nature.

*Tip* Don't make the mistake I made once. *Always* make sure you purchase the *white* computer-ready fabric sheets, instead of the off-white option. The colors will be brighter and clearer when you print.

When you can't print a digital photo as large as you would like on your home printer, there is still a solution. For example, when I photographed my dog, Blondie, for my quilt *Precious Moments with Blondie* (page 72), I wanted a larger image of her printed to use in the quilt. I went to my local office supply store and had her photograph enlarged to the size

I wanted and printed on paper. Using Pattern-Ease, a lightweight, polyester nonwoven tracing material that Laura Heine uses in her marvelous collage quilts, I was able to trace the enlarged image of Blondie onto the Pattern-Ease and build my design of Blondie directly onto it. Instead of fusing fabrics like Laura does, I used Roxanne Glue-Baste-It, a Roxanne Glue Stick, and a repositionable spray adhesive (page 8) to position my fabrics into place. The Pattern-Ease actually became part of the quilt.

I had issues with Blondie's face not looking realistic, so I decided to refer back to the original photo that I took of her. I cropped Blondie's face in the original photo and saved it as a file. Next, I enlarged her face and played around with the correct scale, printing her face on regular printer paper in gray tone, until I got the scale correct. Then, I printed her face in color on a fabric sheet and attached her face and head to the rest of the body.

## Online Printing

One of the easiest ways to incorporate a digital image or to use an image as a quilt top is to send the image to a commercial online company that enlarges and prints images on fabric up to a certain size. My favorite site to send an image to online is Spoonflower (see Supplies and Resources, page 124). My favorite fabric choice that they offer is the organic cotton sateen because of the lovely sheen. Generally speaking, I recommend ordering the fat quarter–size option. I use the camera on my smartphone in "pro" mode to capture an image and then load it onto Spoonflower's site to be enlarged and printed. Spoonflower will print the image on the fabric of your choice and ship it back to you.

When Spoonflower sends back the enlarged and printed image, you have many options for using it. You can add free-motion embroidery to add texture, or you can enhance it with paints, inks, wax pastels, or other "painterly" products, or you can just sandwich and quilt it. It is perfect as a memory quilt, as demonstrated in my quilt *Mt. Rainier*. This is one of my favorite places on earth and when I go there, I just sit and stare at the mountain for hours and I consider it a spiritual haven. The photograph of Mt. Rainier was taken by Dan Neil and sent to Spoonflower for printing. For the finished quilt and instructions, see *Mt. Rainier* (page 79).

## Mirror-Image Digital Photographs

In my quilt *Mt. Rainier Reflecting in Tipsoo Lake* (page 88), there is a mirror image of Mt. Rainier and trees reflecting into the lake. In order to have a mirror image, I created the original Mt. Rainier separately and added the colored glacier areas prior to actually placing it in the design on my working wall. Next, I took a close-up photo of the mountain and placed it into a photo file on my computer. I adjusted the size of the mountain so that it was just a tiny bit smaller than the original mountain and then I printed it on computer-ready fabric using the mirror-image command on my printer.

Original photograph of Mt. Rainier

Photo by Dan Neil

## Mirror-Image Trees

For the mirror image of the trees, I didn't use a digital image. To create the trees and their reflections, I measured how tall and wide my trees would be and then I doubled the fabric I needed for the length, plus an extra inch or two. Next, I folded the fabric in half wrong side out and with the fold on the bottom. I drew each tree on computer paper and glued it to the fabric with the bottom of the tree next to the fold. *Without cutting through the fold*, I cut each set of trees out individually, turned them right side up, and numbered them using painter's tape. Each tree and its reflection had the same number. Once they were all cut, I cut through the fold line and I had the tree and its exact mirror reflection.

When positioning reflections, they are always a bit shorter due to the land in the middle. See the completed quilt *Mt. Rainier Reflecting in Tipsoo Lake* (page 88).

Creating mirror image trees

## Needle Lace or Seafoam

I love beach scenes with foamy water and waves, but I wasn't sure how to capture that realism in my quilts. In the past, I found fabrics that I could use but I wanted something with more texture and realism. Again, it boiled down to trial and error to find the answer. I finally tried creating a needle lace of sorts on a boil-away stabilizer. I used my method of creating needle lace for foamy waves in my quilt *Paradise* (page 109), combining it with commercial wave-like fabrics. The *Aloha Spirit* pattern (page 82) demonstrates how to create the needle lace.

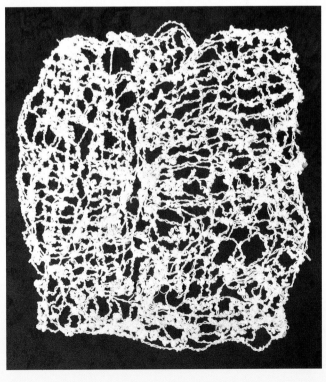

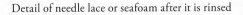

Detail of needle lace or seafoam after it is rinsed

## Creating Exposed Bricks on a Wall

In *Melanie's Quilt* (page 114), I created a garden, and on the right side
of the garden wall where the sun is
shining, my goal was to expose part of
the bricks. I had no idea how to make
the exposed bricks look realistic, so I
tried several techniques. Eventually, I
decided to create the tiny bricks using
the same fabric that the wall is made
from, but I positioned part of them on
a fabric that reads like a brick mortar.
Since the bricks are quite small, I cut
them individually with my small rotary
cutter, sprayed them individually with
glue, and placed them on the fabric using Heidi Proffetty's Precision Tweezers
to get the correct placement. Once I
had a section of the exposed brick wall
completed, I cut the outside edges to
look rough and old and glued it on top
of the original wall fabric.

Detail of the exposed brick on right side of
*Melanie's Quilt* (full quilt, page 114)

## Take a Risk

When I created my quilt *Fantasy Forest* (page 90), I studied the hand-dyed background fabric for probably a year before my mind told me what to do with it. When studying the fabric, it seemed like the sun was breaking through the darkness of the forest in the upper left-hand side. When I saw a *National Geographic* magazine photo of towering redwood trees with sunbeams filtering through, I knew I had my answer. My design needed sunbeams.

Again, I just put my thinking cap on, trying to visualize how to accomplish my goal. I began trials with different fabrics for the sunbeams, such as silk organza, regular organza, bridal illusion tulle, sheer voile, and netting, all with no success. Eventually, I found a white fabric that was a cross between bridal illusion tulle and netting, and it was sturdy enough for me to weave between and behind the trees. My goal with the sunbeams was to have them appear like they converged at a vanishing point in the distance in the upper left corner of the design. Not all sunbeams are the same size, so I cut my sunbeams with different widths using my rotary cutter and ruler.

Placing my in-progress design on a table, the next step in the process was to weave the sunbeams in front of and behind the trees. At this point, I had not basted my design. Since I used a repositionable spray adhesive (page 8) on the redwood trees, I was able to individually lift each one and reposition it once a sunbeam was intertwined in place. Once the redwoods and the sunbeams were positioned, I basted them to my canvas with monofilament thread.

Sometimes it's good to step away from what we think is right or wrong when selecting fabrics for a landscape quilt. Again, it all boils down to taking risks. In my quilt *Kitty in the Garden* (page 98), I couldn't find a fabric in my stash that I felt would work well as the garden wall. I tried all sorts of typical landscape wall fabrics, but none of them spoke to me. Thumbing through my hand-dyed and hand-painted fabrics, I came across a fabric that I wouldn't ordinarily use in a landscape quilt, but something in me said, "Give it a shot, Joyce." I auditioned the hand-painted abstract fabric as the wall in the design, and it just clicked. Sometimes, the small differences in your landscape quilts end up helping with the overall success of the visual effect.

Detail of abstract garden wall in *Kitty in the Garden* (full quilt, page 98)

# Adding a Border to an Already-Quilted Quilt

Chapter Seven (page 58) discusses border options for landscape quilts. There have been times after I have designed a quilt when I have said to myself, "This quilt doesn't need a border," so I've gone ahead and quilted it. Then, I am disappointed afterward because I think the quilt really does need a border. No worries; it is possible to add a border after the quilt is done. Here is a photo of a quilt that originally had no borders.

Nightglow in Hawaii *without borders*

Nightglow in Hawaii *with borders, by Joyce R. Becker, Kent, Washington, 25" × 27", 2020*

To add borders after a quilt has been blocked, squared, and bound, here is the process:

## Materials and Supplies

*Yardage is based on 40" of usable fabric width unless otherwise noted. Quantities noted are enough for a quilt that is up to 34" × 40" before adding these borders.*

**Front border and binding:** ¾ yard

**Back borders and sleeve (same as quilt backing):** ¾ yard

**Threads:** To match top and back borders

**Repositionable spray adhesive:** I used 505 Temporary Adhesive for Fabric (by Odif).

**Thin batting:** ½ yard (I used Hobbs Thermore Batting.)

## Cutting

**Front borders:** Cut 2 strips 2½" × length of quilt and 2 strips 2½" × width of quilt plus 5".

**Binding:** Cut 5 strips 2½" × width of fabric.

**Back borders:** Cut 2 strips 2½" × length of quilt and 2 strips 2½" × width of quilt plus 5".

**Sleeve:** Cut 1 strip 8½" × *new* width of quilt plus 2".

**Thin batting:** Cut 4 strips 2½" × length of quilt and 4 strips 2½" × width of quilt plus 5".

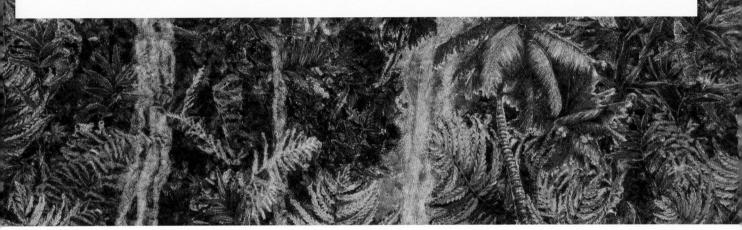

## Construction

**1.** Remove the binding from the quilt.

**2.** Square the quilt again.

 **You may need to undo some of the quilting to have access to sew on the front and back borders.**

**3.** Instead of mitered borders, use a square border format. Use a ¼" presser foot to sew the borders to the left and right sides of the front of the quilt.

**4.** Press the seams.

**5.** Repeat Step 3 to sew the side borders to the back of the quilt.

**6.** Press the seams.

**7.** Glue and position 2 layers of batting into each border sandwich.

 **Use 2 layers of batting so that the border will be the same weight as the rest of the quilt after it is quilted.**

**8.** Repeat Steps 3–7 for the top and bottom border strips on the front and back of the quilt.

**9.** Quilt the border using a meandering stitch.

**10.** Square the quilt again.

**11.** Add the binding and a sleeve.

**12.** If desired, add a trim or a braid around the inner edges of the borders (see *Night Glow in Hawaii*, page 105).

## Using Your Printer to Create Fabric

There are times in life when you just have to come up with a solution to a problem because of time constraints. When I was creating a quilt with palm trees on it, I needed one more palm tree, but I ran out of fabric. So, what was my solution? I placed a palm tree I already had cut out on the bed of my printer and then I copied and printed it on computer-ready fabric.

Another time, I was on a deadline and I had the perfect sky fabric for my design, but guess what … I needed another 4″ for my sky, and I was desperate. So I placed the original sky fabric onto my printer bed, and I copied and printed it onto computer-ready fabric.

*Tip* **When joining fabrics together, like the sky and the copied and printed sky fabric, here's what to do. Cut one of the edges of the two fabrics in a wavy line. Overlap the fabric with the wavy line on top of the other fabric, and glue it with repositionable glue. If you join them with a straight line, your eye will always go to the straight line, whereas you won't notice a wavy line.**

A palm tree copied onto computer-ready cotton fabric

# Embellishments and Other Fun Stuff

## Coloring Tools

Having an assortment or collection of coloring options in your studio is a true blessing. You can start out small and add items as your budget allows. I started out with a large collection of Prismacolor artist colored pencils that I purchased at a big box store. Next, I graduated to textile paints, and then on to Tsukineko inks, their Fabrico markers, and Caran d'Ache wax pastels. I actually don't have a favorite medium in that I use whatever is appropriate at the time.

> **Tip** Regardless of the application, *always* heat-set any coloring tool or medium you use once it is dry. *Don't use steam*; use a dry iron. If you are worried, use a pressing cloth or a nonstick pressing sheet over the application of color when you heat-set it.

### *Fabric Choices for All Coloring Mediums*

When you use coloring mediums, consider purchasing white cotton sateen fabric because the sheen from the fabric often shows through the medium and gives the fabric a lovely glow. Many artists prefer painting on a PFD (prepared-for-dyeing) fabric, and that is certainly another option, or you can paint on a white muslin fabric. However, you need to make sure that the muslin is a tightly woven, high-quality muslin. Not all quilting shops carry the cotton sateen or PFD fabrics (see Supplies and Resources, page 124).

The cotton sateen fabric is optically whitened and 45″ wide. The PFD is a Kona cotton that comes in both 45″ and 60″ widths and it is usually 60 threads per inch. In my quilt *Aloha Spirit* (page 82), I used translucent textile paints and painted on cotton sateen fabrics. If you are using a dark-colored medium, such as an opaque textile paint, it is not necessary to use a white cotton sateen fabric as the glow will not come forward.

Chapter Six: Embellishments and Other Fun Stuff     **45**

## *Prismacolor Artists Colored Pencils*

When I first began creating landscape quilts and I didn't have many coloring mediums, I used the Prismacolor artists pencils quite often for coloring and highlighting. The larger the set, the more color and value options you have. Depending upon how much pressure you apply with the pencils, you can get anything from a very fine application of color to a more intense color. Seen in the quilt detail of *The Smoky Mountains* (below), I applied a light touch of a light gray colored pencil on the furthest row of mountains in the distance. On the next row of mountains coming forward, I used a slightly darker value of gray. Since the values of the fabrics I used are so close, I needed the definition between the rows of mountains so they wouldn't blend together

I also used colored pencils to change the colors of a palm tree in my quilt *Aloha Spirit* (detail at right). The tree was originally green, and I wanted to add a little pizzazz to it and make it more interesting.

Detail of palm tree in *Aloha Spirit* (full quilt, page 82), altered with colored pencils

Distant gray mountains in *The Smoky Mountains* (full quilt, page 94) with edges highlighted with Prismacolor artist pencils

## Textile Paints

When painting with textile paints, use a transparent textile paint, if possible, unless you plan on painting dark colors. Excellent choices include Pebeo Setacolor Fabric Paints and PRO Chemical & Dye's PROfab Transparent Textile Paints. Both of these are *transparent* textile paints that you can use both for hand painting and sun printing. If you are painting a dark value, you will need an *opaque* textile paint. It is also fun to add a pearlescent-type textile paint if you want to add a shiny appearance to your painted elements. Lumiere Paint by Jacquard adds a metallic or shiny look for darker elements that you paint.

## Textile Paint Extender

I also recommend purchasing a textile paint extender which allows you to stretch your fabric paints further. The extender can also be mixed with textile fabric paints to thin the paint or when you mix colors. Jacquard makes a good extender. PRO Chemical & Dye also has a very good extender and a pearlescent textile paint extender.

## Mixing Textile Paints

Depending on how much water you use when mixing your paint, your paint color can go from a very intense color to a pale pastel. Most of the time, I don't mix my textile paints with water, I just add the extender so my paint will cover more and last longer before drying out. Sometimes, you won't be able to find the exact color you want, so what then? Try mixing colors together to see if you can get just the shade that you want. I often add white paint to lighten the colors of textile paints. It is important to mix your paints on a palette to get out all of the bumps and lumps. If you don't have a palette, use a piece of glass from a picture frame that you no longer use. You can also use a paper or foam plate; they work just fine. A palette knife for mixing paints is nice, but if you don't have one of those, you can use a plastic knife.

There are many great books available that explain how to use textile paint on fabric and how to mix paints to get a specific color. *Fabric Painting with Cindy Walter* is a good option (see Supplies and Resources, page 124).

## Protecting Painting Surfaces

Always paint your fabric on a protected surface that doesn't have any lumps or bumps underneath. You can use plastic drop cloths available at most home improvement stores, or you can purchase a thicker vinyl at most craft stores. Use clamps on the sides of the table to secure the drop cloth or vinyl. When the weather cooperates, it's nice to paint outside on a protected table. Be aware that it is difficult to paint outside when it is really windy or if it is a hot day because the paint dries very quickly. Sometimes, the garage is a better alternative. I don't advise painting fabric in your studio simply because you risk getting paint on your design table or your floor.

 **Always wear old clothes and surgical gloves when you paint as paint splatters.**

## Paintbrushes

As far as paint applicators go, there are many options including paintbrushes, sponge rollers, sponge brushes, sea sponges, and so forth. I recommend fine brushes for very detailed painting; but otherwise, if you are painting large surfaces such as in my quilt *Aloha Spirit* (page 82), you can use a large inexpensive paintbrush from the home improvement store or a large sponge brush. I also recommend using cut up sea sponges for painting snow on mountains and waves in the ocean.

## Opaque Textile Paint

There are times when you need an opaque-type textile paint, especially when you are painting dark colors. An opaque paint covers the white fabric, and the white fabric doesn't bleed through to the surface.

Here is a sampling of the types of paints, brushes, and painting products I use.

A sampling of textile paints, brushes, and painting products

## Fabrico Markers

Many quilters already have a set of fabric markers. There are those markers, however, that are not so dependable, and they often seem to dry up as soon as you get them home from the store. Fabrico Markers, made by Tsukineko, use the same ink as in their all-purpose inks, and depending on how much you use them, they can last for years. Markers are excellent for highlighting areas that you want to pop or for shading. Markers are especially good to use when you want shading and marking on trees. In my quilt *Quaking Aspens—Fall* (detail below), I used the markers to shade and accent the aspen trees.

 I also like to use the fabric markers to change the color of flowers or leaves. Starch your fabric first and do the coloring *before* you cut out the flowers or leaves, it is much easier.

Shading with a Fabrico Marker on aspen trees in *Quaking Aspens—Fall* (full quilt, page 101)

## Tsukineko All-Purpose Inks

Tsukineko inks are a remarkable product. They are entirely different from textile paints in that they are very fluid and spread easily but I have used them over the years in many of my quilts. In *Fantasy Forest* (detail below), for example, I had a very limited amount of the original redwood tree fabric, only enough for the trees in the foreground. I have almost every color of the Tsukineko inks, so I blended colors to come up with the appropriate color to match the other trees. I painted a large piece of cotton sateen fabric with the inks, let it dry, heat-set it, and then cut the trees out with my rotary equipment. I have also painted entire borders for some of my quilts because I couldn't find the color or value of fabric that I wanted. These high-quality inks can be used with Tsukineko's special applicators or foam or paintbrushes.

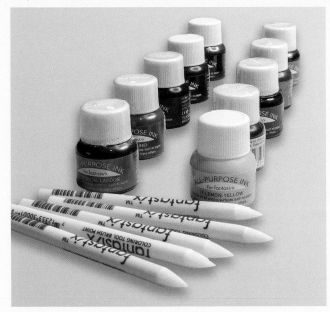

Tsukineko inks and applicators

Detail of redwood trees in the background painted with Tsukineko inks in *Fantasy Forest* (full quilt, page 90)

Detail of the sky in *Mt. Rainier Reflecting in Tipsoo Lake* (full quilt, page 88)

## Caran D'Ache Neocolor II Water Soluble Wax Pastels

If I were to pick one product that I truly love and use the most, it would be these amazing wax pastels. Yes, they look like crayons, but they are so much more. You can blend them to create a mix of colors and values, and they have a lovely sheen or luminosity that appears on the surface. Just like some other mediums, the intensity of color that you get on your fabric depends on how much pressure you apply. You can use the wax pastels on wet or dry fabric or blend colors either way.

 **Tip** After you apply the wax pastels, use your finger to smear the color and the luminosity becomes more apparent. When you want to blend two or more colors, dampen a piece of muslin to mix the colors together.

In the quilt detail of *Mt. Rainier Reflecting in Tipsoo Lake* (above), I painted the sky and water with translucent textile paints. Once the paint was dry and heat-set, I added the areas of the pink in the sky and water with wax pastels to implicate that it was morning. I used my smear technique and a dampened cloth to blend two different colors together.

# Other Fun Embellishments and Found Items

## *Angelina*

I've talked about using Angelina in my previous books, but this time I used it in two separate applications. Angelina fibers are iridescent ultra-fine synthetic fibers that reflect and refract light, giving a beautiful shimmering effect. Angelina is wonderful when used in water or as ice. In most cases, you will create a sheet of bonded Angelina fibers for those purposes. Angelina actually bonds to itself when heated with an iron on a nonstick pressing sheet.

For bonded Angelina, arrange the fibers together on top of a nonstick pressing sheet so there are no stringy looking areas. Place another nonstick pressing sheet above the Angelina when you bond it. Using a medium heat on an iron, no steam, press across the surface of the nonstick sheet at a pretty fast clip and maintain the same pressure with your iron the whole time. Wait until the Angelina cools down to open up the sheet and see the results.

 If you apply too much heat, your sheet of Angelina will not shimmer or shine. If you apply too little heat, Angelina won't bond to itself.

An example of a bonded Angelina can be seen in the quilt detail of *Mt. Rainier Reflecting in Tipsoo Lake* (below). I used Angelina to divide the picture and the reflection apart.

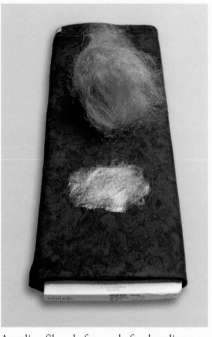

Angelina fibers before and after bonding

Detail of bonded Angelina in *Mt. Rainier Reflecting in Tipsoo Lake* (full quilt, page 88)

## Capturing Angelina

You can also use the Angelina without bonding, but you must capture it under something because when the fibers are loose, they fly around and stick to everything. In *Precious Moments with Blondie* (page 72), I placed loose green Angelina on top of a commercial water fabric to make the water appear like it was shining and shimmering. Next, I placed a layer of matching green tulle over the top of the Angelina to hold it in place, and I followed up by basting the Angelina and tulle into place with dark gray monofilament thread.

Detail of "captured" Angelina on the water in *Precious Moments with Blondie* (full quilt, page 72)

## Unusual Embellishments

Today, you can see various collage portraits of animals, especially cats and dogs, in quilting books, magazines, and on social media. My goal when creating *Precious Moments with Blondie* (page 72) was to include my beloved cocker spaniel, Blondie. I tried about a bazillion things before I was happy with the results. As I mentioned in Chapter Five, Printing at Home (page 36), I took a photograph of Blondie and I took it to my local office supply store and had it enlarged and printed on paper. I traced the enlarged image onto a product called Pattern-Ease. I built Blondie's body on top of the traced image using many mediums.

First, I tried building Blondie with just fabrics, but I didn't like the result. Next, I tried several other combinations of fabrics and started adding other stuff like unraveled yarns, commercial fur fabrics, and believe it or not, fur that my husband saved from Blondie when he groomed her. With all those layers of different fibers, I ended up placing a layer of tulle over Blondie's whole body, except for the ears, and stitched her separately from the quilt.

 You don't need to remove Pattern-Ease; it acts as an interfacing or stabilizer.

As far as Blondie's head went, I didn't like anything that I produced. I actually made the head separately from the body because I wanted to use the actual printed photograph as a basis for her face, especially her eyes. In order to do that, I found the original photograph of Blondie and I printed it on paper. Next, I cut away the head from the photograph and began enlarging her head on my printer until I got the right size. Next I printed Blondie's head on a fabric sheet for my inkjet printer. I added other accents to her face including shading with wax pastels and an overlay of tulle and then I stitched her head to the body. Next, I raw-edge appliquéd Blondie to the actual quilt.

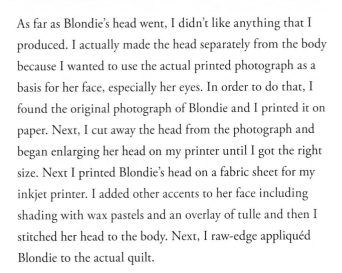

Original photograph of Blondie and Blondie traced onto Pattern-Ease and constructed

Blondie's head

## Whatever Works!

After experimenting with other options, I finally settled on using shredded batting to create the waterfalls on my quilt *Night Glow in Hawaii* (see detail on the right). I tried using organza, cheesecloth, yarns, you name it, I tried it. I felt painting the waterfalls would be too static and would look unnatural, so the shredded batting worked the best.

## Crystals and Beads

Sometimes, it's just fun to add something to your quilt that sparkles. I felt like my quilt *A Winter's Night* (page 107) needed something else to make it pop, so I added clear fusible Swarovski crystals in the sky. I ordered a box with several sizes to select from. Make sure to follow the instructions to get the best results.

Detail of the sky in *A Winter's Night* (full quilt, page 107)

## Overlays

We have already discussed how to use overlays of tulle in many of my quilts. Overlays are important in landscape quilts, especially when you want to change the value of the fabrics to help create the correct perspective in your quilts. You may find that there are times when your quilt design is done but there is a little voice in your head saying, "Something just isn't right." In the case of my quilt *Night Glow in Hawaii* (page 105), when I looked at my finished design, there just seemed to be too many elements that were strung together that didn't jell, and the whole quilt just seemed to be too busy. When looking at my design, my eye would try and stop on each individual palm tree or bush instead of flowing across the whole design. The answer to my dilemma was to put an overlay of dark blue tulle over the entire surface of the design except for the sky. The tulle also added to the mood of the piece, focusing on a nighttime scene.

Detail of a waterfall in *Night Glow in Hawaii* (full quilt, page 105)

## Chapter Seven

# Free-Motion Embroidery, Borders, and Quilting Options

## Free-Motion Embroidery

Adding free-motion embroidery to your quilt when it is still a top is a terrific option if you plan on adding a lot of density and texture to your quilt. When you incorporate raw-edge free-motion embroidery on a quilt top, you can use almost any type of thread that quilters typically use that will enhance the design. If you want density in your elements or you want to fill in a shape quickly, a thicker thread, such as a 30- or 12-weight cotton thread, works well. One of my favorite threads for free-motion embroidery is 30-weight Sulky Blendables cotton thread. Some quilters refer to these types of threads as *variegated threads*. These threads add a lot of texture quickly and Sulky provides many variations of color combinations.

When you do a large portion of the thread work while your quilt is just the top, it doesn't matter what the back of your quilt top looks like because no one will ever see it. If you prefer a regular cotton thread, Sulky 50-weight (which includes the Cotton + Steel line of threads) is perfect for accomplishing free-motion raw-edge appliqué as well. I also use many of the cotton varieties of WonderFil Specialty Threads in my designs.

*Tip* After you have basted your quilt top, take it to your local quilt shop and audition threads to accomplish your machine embroidery and quilting so you can find the perfect color and value match. Not all your quilts will need this option, but others seem to beg for it.

Assortment of Sulky threads: Blendables 30-weight threads (*front*) and Cotton + Steel 50-weight cotton threads (*back box*)

When you accomplish free-motion machine embroidery, you *do not* have to start in the middle of the quilt and work out like you do when you are quilting your quilt. For example, in *Mt. Rainier Reflecting in Tipsoo Lake* (page 88), I did the dense machine embroidery on all the trees first, using a matching cotton 30-weight Sulky thread. You can see the difference the free-motion raw-edge machine embroidery makes in the trees below. The first tree shown has no free-motion raw-edge embroidery, while the second tree does.

Tree without free-motion embroidery

For this type of tree to appear dense and pop out, a circular stitch and a thick 30-weight cotton thread was used. Here is an example of the free-motion embroidery stitch:

Circular stitch to create density

Douglas fir trees in *Mt. Rainier Reflecting in Tipsoo Lake* (full quilt, page 88) with dense free-motion embroidery

In my quilt *Majestic Mountains* (page 67), most of the stitching on the grasses in the foreground was done in the free-motion machine embroidery stage, and I used a straight stitch with a 30-weight Sulky Blendables cotton thread.

Detail of *Majestic Mountains* (full quilt, page 67) raw-edge machine embroidery stitching on the tall grass in the foreground

## Thread Choices

It's fun to play with a variety of threads, from different weights to threads that are blendable or variegated, through choices like polyester, rayon, cotton, or silk. When you shop, try to find the perfect color and value thread that is spot on for your particular design. Even though I probably have somewhere between 150 to 200 spools of green thread, it seems like there are times when none of my green threads will work. My husband thinks I am certifiably nuts when I speed off to the quilt shop for more thread, considering what's already in my studio.

## Bobbin Thread

My favorite bobbin thread is WonderFil's InvisaFil thread (see Supplies and Resources, page 124). It is also wonderful for appliqué, feels like silk, is 100-weight, and comes in 60 different colors. Being able to match your top thread with your bobbin thread is remarkable because you will never see the little "dot" of thread that pops to the top of your quilt when your thread tension balance is anything but perfect. You can also use the InvisaFil thread in the bobbin when you are quilting if you don't want your stitches to show very much on the back of the quilt. Just select a thread that matches your backing fabric. When possible, use an InvisaFil matching bobbin thread when you are accomplishing your raw-edge machine embroidery.

*Tip* Some thicker threads, such as 12- and 30-weights, don't always play nicely with a lighter-weight bobbin thread, so you *may* need to consider using a matching 40- or 50-weight thread instead. Try to match the color of both threads if possible.

Some quilts really don't need free-motion machine embroidery. For example, if you are going to be creating one of the quilts in this book using the technique in *Quick Little Landscape Quilt*, you will use a thick stabilizer (such as fast-2fuse Heavy Interfacing, by C&T Publishing) to build your design on, and the process differs from a regular landscape quilt. Your design will have no backing or batting and it will be placed in a picture frame. All your stitching is done at the quilting stage after you baste your quilt.

On some quilts, such as *A Winter's Night* (page 107), there wasn't any reason to include machine embroidery. It's a faraway scene with no focal points, so adding another layer or dimension to it is truly unnecessary. I did, however, add quite a dense layer of quilting throughout this quilt.

Examples of WonderFil's
InvisaFil bobbin thread

## Pressing Your Quilt Top

Once you have finished the raw-edge machine embroidery on your quilt top it is time to press your quilt top *from the back*. Why not press your quilt top from the front? Actually, there are several reasons. When you baste your quilt, you typically use a transparent monofilament thread on the top of the quilt, and some transparent threads melt. Also, if you used any kind of coloring medium on your quilt and you forgot to heat-set your quilt top, the colors may run. Or what if your iron doesn't want to cooperate and spews out rusty water on your quilt top?

Heat your iron to medium-high with steam and place your quilt facedown on your ironing board. Your goal is to steam out any puckers that may have been caused by the dense raw-edge machine embroidery. Don't worry if you are stretching your quilt top out of shape; you will be squaring your quilt soon.

*Tip* **If the quilt top still seems to pucker, take a snip with your tiny scissors through the muslin to release the lump. Don't cut your quilt top, though!**

Snip through the muslin to remove puckers

## Squaring a Quilt Top

If you decide you want to add borders to your quilt after you have completed the free-motion machine embroidery on your quilt top, you will need to square your quilt first. For basic instructions, see Squaring (page 58).

## Borders

### To Border or Not?

If my husband had his way, he would say, "Yes, your quilt needs a border." I, however, do not feel the same. Some quilts scream for a border and others just say, "I'm done, I don't need a border!" If you are not sure whether to add a border to a quilt, here are some suggestions:

**1.** Audition your quilt on your working wall with a variety of possible border fabrics and then take photos.

**2.** Next, take a photo of the quilt top without a border.

**3.** Now it is time to listen to that little voice in your head. It will tell you which option to choose.

**4.** If you absolutely can't decide between possible border fabrics or whether to put a border on your quilt or not, ask a couple of your quilting buddies what they think. After you make a few landscape quilts, the option to add a border or not will come more naturally.

## Facing and Binding Alternatives

You have a choice of placing a border on your quilt top or adding a facing or binding once your quilt is complete. There are times when adding a border or even a binding can take away from the visual interest of a quilt. Here is an example of a quilt that is faced versus having binding or borders (see Binding or Facing?, page 120).

A Winter's Night *with a facing*

### *Fabric Choices for Borders*

Fabric choices for borders are very important. You want the border on your quilt to enhance your design, not distract from it. Fabrics with a bit of movement are nice choices for borders. Many times, solid fabrics are too static, and your eye will go straight to the border instead of the actual quilt. A good rule of thumb is to go one shade darker than the darkest value in your quilt for a border choice.

 If your eye goes directly to the border instead of the quilt, it's the wrong fabric.

Examples of suitable border fabrics

## Double Border Choices

Sometimes, it's actually fun to add a border or borders that give the quilt a jump of enthusiasm. For example, in the quilt *Kitty in the Garden* (page 98) I actually added two borders that added more visual interest to the design. The small striped inner border really stops the busy action of the quilt center. The outer border gives a calming look to the design and makes it more cohesive.

Detail of borders for *Kitty in the Garden* (full quilt, page 98)

## Adding a Border

Add your border(s) after you have basted your quilt, finished the raw-edge machine embroidery, pressed your quilt from the back, and squared your quilt. For step-by-step instructions, see Chapter Eleven (page 117).

### Sizing Borders

I always audition the fabrics I am considering for my landscape quilts next to my quilt top. Once I have determined which fabric is suitable, I audition how large I want my borders to be. You don't want the quilt borders to overtake the quilt, just to enhance it. Start by auditioning a 3½″-wide border which will end up as a 3″ border. Try a larger and a smaller size border until you are satisfied. Cut all the borders the same width and add at least an extra 2″ in length if you want to miter the corners.

## Mitering Corners

We all have different preferences when it comes to mitering or not mitering the corners of the borders we add to our quilts. Some of you may prefer doing square corners while others may have their own particular method of mitering the border corners. Here is a slick way to miter quilt corners:

**1.** Stitch the side borders onto the quilt top first, stopping ¼″ from each corner.

**2.** Stitch the top and the bottom borders onto the quilt, again stopping ¼″ from each corner.

**3.** At each corner, fold one side to create a 45° angle.

Fold to create a 45° angle

**4.** Finger press the fold line and then press with a dry iron.

**5.** Flip the mitered edge back and spray it with repositionable spray adhesive (page 8). Position a piece of cardboard or paper under the edge as shown.

Flip the mitered edge back and glue

**6.** Position the folded and sprayed border back into place and once it is dry, press it with a dry iron.

**7.** Using a matching or monofilament thread and a blind hem stitch, stitch along the fold line. Trim the mitered seam allowances to ¼″ after stitching.

Blind-stitched mitered border corner

**Tip** In order for the borders to be the same weight as the rest of the quilt and not flop around, stabilize your border strips with the same fusible interfacing you used on your canvas. Depending upon the weight of the top of the quilt and all the layers of fabric, you will normally need to add at least two layers of the interfacing in your borders. Do not put the interfacing in the seam allowance.

Stabilize quilt borders with interfacing

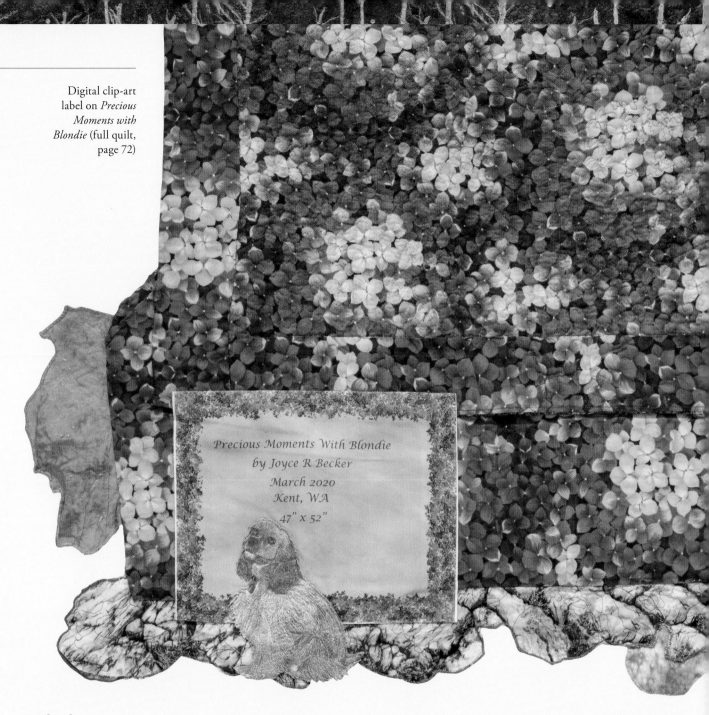

Digital clip-art label on *Precious Moments with Blondie* (full quilt, page 72)

Precious Moments With Blondie
by Joyce R Becker
March 2020
Kent, WA
47" x 52"

## Labels

Before you begin the quilting process, I suggest you make a label for the back of your quilt. Be sure to include the title of your quilt, your name, where you live, the date, and if you are entering a competition, your telephone number.

If you would like to create your own label, take a photo of your quilt with a digital camera and load the image into the photo program on your computer. You can play around with the appropriate size that you want your image to be and then leave space below your image for the vital statistics. Leave room to turn the edges under so that they are not raw-edge, or, if you wish, cut the edges with a serrated rotary cutter. A 5″ × 7″ label is a good size. Attach your label to the bottom left corner on the quilt back, pinning or basting lightly into place before you quilt.

*Tip* **After having a quilt stolen, I try to stitch my label onto my quilt during the quilting stage. I use transparent monofilament thread when attaching the label to the quilt back. Many clip-art labels are also available for free on the internet; just search "free quilt labels." I used free clip-art for the label on *Precious Moments with Blondie* (page 72) and added a thread-painted Blondie just for fun.**

# Quilting

When you are ready to quilt your quilt, I recommend Hobbs Thermore Batting and a good-quality backing fabric versus a backing with a low thread count. If you want your stitches to show, use a solid color backing. If you don't, use a patterned fabric and a monofilament or InvisaFil matching thread in the bobbin.

## Steps for Sandwiching

1. Cut your backing fabric a few inches larger than your design.

2. Lay the backing fabric wrong side up on a protected flat surface.

3. Secure the backing with painter's tape on all 4 corners to keep it from shifting.

4. To help remove the wrinkles in the batting, try placing it in a clothes dryer on the "no heat" or "air" setting.

5. Cut your batting a few inches larger than your quilt top and fold in half.

6. Place the folded batting on the backing with the fold at the center of the backing.

7. Spray repositionable spray adhesive (page 8) on the wrong side of exposed half of the backing fabric and unfold the batting, gently positioning it in place.

8. Fold the half of the batting without adhesive up and repeat Step 7 for the other half.

9. Fold the quilt top in half, right sides together. Place the top on the batting with the fold at the center.

10. Spray the adhesive on the exposed half of the batting and gently lay the quilt top into place.

11. Fold the half of the quilt top without adhesive up and repeat Step 10 for the other half.

12. Check the back and front of the quilt to make sure there are no puckers. You can still lift away the backing or your quilt top to smooth it into place.

13. Let the adhesive dry and you are ready to quilt.

## Hoops and Gloves

Some of you may prefer using gloves, hoops, and such, during the machine embroidery and quilting stages. My preference is to control the fabric and the way it moves myself.

## Good Body Position When Quilting

The height of your sewing machine and table should be at a 90° angle when you put your arms straight ahead. When you're sitting at your table, the height should be where your elbows can be bent at a 90° angle and close to your body. You also need to be aware of maintaining good posture during all the stages when you are stitching on your sewing machine. Many of us tend to lean forward while we sew which is terrible for our backs, necks, and shoulders. When you're sitting at your machine and sewing, sit with your shoulders relaxed and your back straight.

Most of your quilting will be done free-motion with the feed dogs down on your sewing machine. If your quilt includes raw-edge appliqué, you will quilt on top of what you have already stitched but not as heavily.

When your quilt is sandwiched you are ready to start the quilting stage. *Always* begin in the middle of the quilt and work outward. Yes, you will have to change threads often. Try to stitch with the same density throughout.

Some quilts are quite busy and really don't need more attention. Such is the case with *A Kitty in the Garden* (page 98). I quilted it mostly by going around each element with a matching thread making sure the density of the quilting was uniform.

Positioning yourself for quilting

## Types of Quilting Stitches

When it is time to quilt your design, you have to ask yourself, "How do I want my design to look?" Do you want to do a lot of quilting or do you want to just enhance your design with the quilting? If you have done a lot of machine embroidery, just quilt on top of it but accomplish the quilting with less density and try to keep it uniform throughout the whole design.

### Receding Quilting

Sometimes, you want your quilting stitches to recede, or drop into the background, such as when quilting the water or sky. To get your stitches to recede, try to match your sky or water threads with the actual background fabric so that the background stays a negative space. Here is an example:

 **Tip** You may find that the raw-edge elements in your design look ragged on the edges because the fabrics have frayed. If that happens, quilt around the frayed elements with a small zigzag stitch with a complementary thread.

Quilting stitch for water and sky

Detail of quilting on hosta and hydrangea plants in *Precious Moments with Blondie* (full quilt, page 72)

## Flowers, Leaves, Bark, and More

Your job, when quilting, is to make your designs look realistic. So when you think about adding in accents with quilting, such as the veins in leaves or enhancing flowers, keep in mind how the object actually looks in nature. The same thing goes for the bark on trees. How does the bark on the particular type of tree you are working on actually look? I often research these types of questions on the internet, finding samples of how the bark looks on a redwood tree, a Douglas fir tree, or an aspen tree, and then I try to emulate that when I accomplish my quilting. Northcott Fabrics has a nice variety of realistic barklike fabrics available. Notice how I have tried to emulate the particular markings on the hosta and the hydrangea plants with my quilting in *Precious Moments with Blondie* (page 72).

## *Quilting Borders*

For quilting the borders on your quilt there are many options. You can try any of these:

• Follow the pattern printed on the fabric, matching the thread to the fabric.

• Stipple stitch the border, using a matching thread.

• Quilt straight lines or a grid, using feed dogs up and a ¼″ foot or embroidery foot.

• Create a quilting pattern that follows a motif from the theme of your landscape design.

## *Adding a Hanging Sleeve*

Most seasoned quilters already know how to add a hanging sleeve to the back of a quilt once it is completed. My method is to cut an 8½″ strip to make a 4″ tube sleeve using the same fabric as my backing fabric. I attach it approximately ½″ below the top edge of the quilt, stitching both edges by hand with matching thread.

## Chapter Eight

# Join the Digital Age

## Majestic Mountains
*Joyce R. Becker, Kent, Washington, 19" × 23", 2017*

## Inspiration and Description

I created this quilt to show as a sample when I appeared on *Quilting Arts TV*. This quilt was inspired by the exquisite mountain fabric that was part of a quilting panel called Mountain Majesties: Spring, Land That I Love, a Digital Print Fabric from Hoffman California Fabrics. I also incorporated part of a second panel for the trees that are underneath the mountain, this one called Botanical Trail: Wildflower Mountain Border, a Digital Print Fabric from Michael Miller Fabrics. Although these two digital fabric panels may no longer be available for purchase, a large variety of digital panels are currently marketed with mountains and trees and so on that are good substitutes to be incorporated into your designs. (See Chapter 3, Digital Prints and Images, page 22.)

The rest of the design includes commercial and hand-dyed fabrics. We are very fortunate to have lovely representational landscape panels to include or use in our landscape quilts these days. Here are the two panels that I used portions of.

Panel 1, Mountain Majesties: Spring, Land That I Love (a Digital Print Fabric from Hoffman California Fabrics)

Panel 2, Botanical Trail: Wildflower Mountain Border (a Digital Print Fabric from Michael Miller Fabrics)

## Materials and Supplies

*Yardage is based on 40″ of usable fabric width unless otherwise noted.*

*Muslin (bleached or not):* ¾ yard

*Interfacing:* Fusible sheer or featherweight (20″ width of fabric), 1½ yards

*Light blue/aqua with clouds:* ½ yard for sky

*Panel 1:* Black, gray, and white mountains, or a scene you prefer

*Panel 2:* Avocado green trees and reflecting trees, or a scene you prefer

*Medium blue/aqua:* ½ yard for water with reflecting clouds
(I used a hand-dyed fabric.)

*Green/avocado:* ½ yard for underlay for all grasses

*Green/avocado (smaller scale):* ½ yard for grasses in distance

*Green/avocado (large scale):* ¾ yard for grasses in foreground
(This amount allows extra for selective cutting.)

*Green/avocado batik (dark):* ¼ yard for darker trees in foreground

*Green/avocado batik (light):* ¼ yard for lighter trees in foreground

*Brown and white print:* ¼–½ yard, depending upon print for deer in foreground

*Red and blue floral print:* ½ yard (or use flowers from panels) for Indian paintbrush and lupine flowers in foreground

*Backing and sleeve:* 1 yard

*Binding:* ⅜ yard (I used an avocado green-striped batik.)

*Threads:*

Monofilament threads: transparent and dark gray
(I used 60-weight Madeira Monofil Clear and Smoke.)

Matching cotton threads
(I used 30-weight Sulky Blendables cotton.)

Matching bobbin threads
(I used InvisaFil.)

*Thin batting:* ¾ yard (I used Hobbs Thermore Batting.)

*Repositionable spray adhesive:* I used 505 Temporary Adhesive for Fabric (by Odif).

*Spray starch*

## Cutting

*Backing:* Cut 1 rectangle 23″ × 27″.

*Sleeve:* Cut 1 strip 8½″ × width of quilt plus 2″.

*Binding:* Cut 3 strips 2½″ × width of fabric.

*Batting:* Cut 1 rectangle 23″ × 27″.

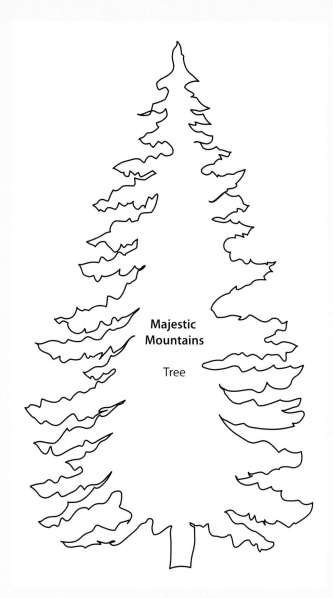

## Prepare the Fabric

**1.** Make a 23″ × 27″ stabilized canvas with the muslin and interfacing. (Refer to Creating a Stabilized Canvas, page 15.)

**2.** Starch all the fabrics except the sky, backing, sleeve, and binding. (Refer to Irons and Starch, page 9.)

## Construction

**1.** Fold your stabilized canvas into thirds and mark with a pencil.

**2.** Place the canvas on your design wall.

**3.** Cut out the sky fabric; glue and position into place.

**4.** Cut out the mountain fabric; glue and position into place.

**5.** Cut out the water fabric; glue and position into place.

**6.** Cut out the tree and tree reflection fabric from the panel; glue and position into place.

**7.** Starch the small grass fabric and cut out the small grass elements; glue and position into place.

**8.** Repeat Step 7 for the large grasses.

**9.** Make a photocopy of the pattern for the larger trees (at right). Make an additional photocopy of the tree pattern, reducing the print size by 15%.

Majestic
Mountains

Tree

Detail of grasses

*Fine Finishing*

**10.** Cut out the patterns. Using 2 layers of the lighter value green fabric and the smaller template, spray the template with glue and position it onto the back of the fabric. Repeat with the larger template and darker value green fabric.

**11.** Cut out the trees, moving the fabric, *not* the scissors. Take your time so that your trees are realistic.

**12.** Glue and position the trees into place.

**13.** Cut out the deer; glue and position into place.

**14.** Cut out the flowers; glue and position into place.

*Tip* **You may need to cut down the flowers to a smaller size, depending upon the scale of the printed fabric.**

**15.** Baste the entire composition with monofilament thread. Use the clear color on the lighter fabrics and the smoke on the darker fabrics. Use a matching bobbin thread.

Free-motion raw-edge machine embroidery really enhances this design. (See Free-Motion Embroidery, page 55.) This is how I machine embroidered mine:

**1.** The trees underneath the mountains and the trees in the foreground were densely embroidered with matching 30-weight cotton thread.

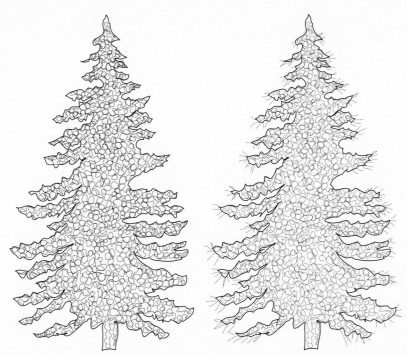

Illustration of raw-edge machine appliqué stitch used on trees

**2.** The small grasses were machine embroidered with a matching 30-weight cotton thread.

**3.** The foreground grasses were machine embroidered with a green 30-weight Sulky Blendables thread.

**4.** Once the raw-edge free-motion embroidery is completed, steam-press the back of the quilt top (see Press Your Quilt Top, page 58).

**5.** Square the quilt top (see Squaring, page 119).

**6.** Sandwich the quilt (see Steps for Sandwiching, page 63).

**7.** Create a label for the quilt (see Labels, page 62) and position it into place.

**8.** Finish the quilting (see Quilting, page 63), block the quilt (see Blocking Your Quilt, page 117), and then square the quilt again.

**9.** Finish the edge (see Binding or Facing?, page 120), and then add a sleeve.

# *Precious Moments with Blondie*

## Quilt Inspiration and Process

This quilt was inspired by the beautiful forest fabric and our sweet cocker spaniel, Blondie. Because I only had a small piece of the forest fabric, I had to cut and piece the forest areas like a puzzle to make it look realistic. I machine appliquéd the forest fabrics together to get the effect I desired.

Creating Blondie was both fun and challenging at the same time. I had her photograph enlarged and traced onto Pattern-Ease to get the desired size. I also created her using a variety of mediums.

The other feature in this design that includes digital imagery was incorporating photographs of the hosta and hydrangea plants in my garden. I uploaded the images I took into a photo-editing program on my computer and enlarged the photographs so they were the correct scale. I then printed them on computer-ready fabric.

I added the fence and the morning glory flowers in the foreground for additional interest and I used a commercial trim for the flower vines.

*Joyce R. Becker,*
*Kent, Washington,*
*47" × 52", 2020*

# Golden Fields

## Quiltmaker Profile and Quilt Inspiration

I had the pleasure of meeting Heidi when we were both guests on the PBS series *Quilting Arts TV*. Watching her during the taping, I was amazed at her expertise using original techniques to create beautiful and unique mosaic creations.

Many times, we artists are inspired to create our art as a result of memories, music, and the beautiful vistas we see around us. For Heidi, she was inspired to make her quilt *Golden Fields* by the Sting song "Fields of Gold," especially a line in the chorus, "…when we walk in fields of gold." When she came across a field that mirrored the picture in her mind of "wheat grass drenched in golden sunshine, quietly, gently swaying," she stopped her car and took a photo of the scene, and she instantly knew it would result in a quilt.

Heidi says she "blends inspirational photography, mosaic design, and quilting with a bit of technology and a digital die-cutting machine to create my mosaic art quilts." Her original art involves many complicated technological steps, which she takes in stride. I shake my head in wonder, trying to understand how she transforms her photographs into drawings with editing software, seeing how she incorporates the appropriate values of fabric into her design and ends up using a digital cutter to create her mosaic quilts.

Heidi's award-winning quilts have won top prizes at the International Quilt Festival in Houston, Texas, and in the American Quilter's Society exhibit in Paducah, Kentucky. In addition to being a guest on *Quilting Arts TV*, Heidi also made a guest appearance on *The Quilt Show* with Alex Anderson and Ricky Tims. She also contributed articles to *Quilting Arts* magazine.

Heidi hopes to continue to enter her art into quilt shows and involve herself in the quilting world with a few more surprises in the future.

*Heidi Proffetty, Bridgewater, Massachusetts, 48½" × 36½", 2020*

Photo by Heidi Proffetty

# Reflections of Frenchman's Mountain in the Wetlands

*Joyce R. Becker, Kent, Washington, 23" × 27", 2020*
From the collection of Barby and Donald Becker Jr.

## Tracing Line Drawings

In this quilt, I needed several things to make the design realistic. The first thing I required was an actual line drawing of the mountain. To accomplish the line drawing, I found a photo of just the mountain online. I printed the image and then took it to my local office supply store and had it enlarged. Next, I traced the line drawing of the mountain onto Pattern-Ease and used one of the stone fabrics from the Stonehenge Gradations collection for Northcott Fabrics for the mountain and the reflection. To create a realistic sky reflection, the clouds in the sky needed to be upside down in the reflection, so I reversed the fabric. I placed a layer of white tulle over the water fabric to calm it down and made the image of the mountain reflection slightly smaller.

## Inspiration and Description

Frenchman's Mountain is located near Las Vegas, Nevada. Our daughter-in-law, Barby, loves looking at the mountain, and when I asked her what kind of landscape scene she would like, she said, "Frenchman's Mountain." After researching the surrounding areas, I found that there is a wetlands under a portion of the mountain, so I decided to incorporate that into the scene.

## Materials and Supplies

*Yardage is based on 40″ of usable fabric width unless otherwise noted.*

**Muslin (bleached or not):** ¾ yard

**Interfacing:** Fusible sheer or featherweight (20″ width of fabric), 1½ yards

**Sky and sky reflection prints:** 1 yard
(I used Light Blue Clouds from Landscape Medley collection for Elizabeth's Studio.)

**Mountain and mountain reflection prints:** 1 yard
(I used Iron Ore from Stonehenge Gradations collection by Linda Ludovico for Northcott Fabrics.)

**Green foliage print:** ½ yard for under mountain
(I used a green from Naturescapes collection by Deborah Edwards for Northcott Fabrics.)

**Light brown, sandlike print:** ½ yard for under rocks and reeds

**Small rock print:** ¼ yard

**Reed print:** 1 yard of fabric that coordinates with green foliage print

**Duck print:** ⅓ yard

**Heron print:** ⅓ yard

**White tulle:** 1 yard for overlay on reflecting mountain and water

**Rust or brown tulle:** ½ yard for overlay on top mountain

**Baby blue tulle:** ¾ yard for overlay on reeds, sand, and rocks

**Turquoise, blue, and green blend print:** 2 yards for border, backing, binding, and sleeve

**Threads:**

Monofilament threads: transparent and dark gray
(I used 60-weight Madeira Monofil Clear and Smoke.)

Matching threads for clouds, mountains, foliage, reeds, rocks, and heron

Matching bobbin thread colors for basting and quilting
(I used InvisaFil.)

**Thin batting:** 1 yard (I used Hobbs Thermore Batting.)

**Repositionable spray adhesive:** I used 505 Temporary Adhesive for Fabric (by Odif).

**Spray starch**

**Optional sparkles:** Irregular shape glitter, multicolor holographic flakes, mylar glitter flakes, rose gold chunky glitter, art acrylic gel

## Cutting

**Border:** Cut 4 strips 3″ × width of fabric.

**Backing:** Cut 1 rectangle 27″ × 31″.

**Binding:** Cut 4 strips 2½″ × width of fabric.

**Sleeve:** Cut 1 strip 8½″ × width of fabric.

**Thin batting:** Cut 1 rectangle 23″ × 27″.

## Prepare the Fabric

**1.** Make a 22″ × 26″ stabilized canvas with the muslin and interfacing. (Refer to Creating a Stabilized Canvas, page 15.)

**2.** Starch all the fabrics except the sky, water, backing, sleeve, and binding. (Refer to Irons and Starch, page 9.)

# Construction

**1.** Place the stabilized and pencil marked canvas on a working wall.

**2.** Cut, glue, and position sky fabric into place.

**3.** Copy the tracing of the mountain on your printer and take it to your local copy store and have it enlarged to 14½″ long by 4½″ wide.

Tracing Frenchman's mountain onto Pattern-Ease

**4.** Trace the line drawing of the mountain onto Pattern-Ease.

**5.** Fold the mountain print in half with the wrong sides together. Draw the mountain shape on the top half of the fabric, using the tracing as your guide.

**6.** Cut just below the drawn line.

**7.** Open up the mountain and the reflection and cut on the fold line. You now have the original mountain and the reflection.

**8.** Glue and position the top mountain on the sky fabric.

**9.** Sprinkle the holographic flakes onto the top mountain, if desired.

**10.** Glue and position the rust/brown tulle overlay on the top mountain.

**11.** Repeat the process for the green foliage, folding the fabric in two, wrong sides together. Cut spiky looking trees on the top edge, using the photograph as your guide.

**12.** Open the fabric and cut along the fold line. You now have the top half and the reflection.

**13.** Glue and position both halves into place.

**14.** Turn the sky fabric that is remaining upside down so it is a reflection.

**15.** Glue and position the upside-down sky fabric into place next to the green foliage fabric.

**16.** Glue and position the reflecting mountain into place.

**17.** Sprinkle a few of the holographic flakes on the reflecting mountain, if desired.

**18.** Glue and position the white tulle over the reflecting foliage, reflecting mountain, and reflecting sky.

**19.** Using the photograph as your guide, cut, glue, and position the sandy fabric along the shorelines as a base for the rocks and the reeds.

**20.** Cut out the ducks, glue, and position them into place.

**21.** Cut out clumps of reeds and rock formations. Cut smaller reed formations for the reeds furthest away in the design. Repeat for the rock formations.

**22.** Start by gluing and positioning the smaller reed and rock formations in the distance first. Continue to come forward in the design, gradually increasing the size of the reeds and rock formations.

**23.** To make your design more interesting in the foreground, position some of the rocks near the shoreline, and others further back on the sandy fabric.

**24.** Cut, glue, and position the blue heron into place. Place the heron among the reeds so she looks natural.

**25.** Cut, glue, and position the baby blue tulle overlay over the reeds, rocks, and heron.

 The reason for the blue tulle overlay is to make it easier to machine quilt the reeds and keep them from raveling or moving when you stitch.

**26.** Baste your design using the dark gray monofilament thread on the mountains and the clear for the rest of the design. Trim away the excess blue tulle that you basted around the reeds and rocks.

## Fine Finishing

**1.** Press the back of the quilt with steam to remove any wrinkles and puckers (see Press Your Quilt Top, page 58).

**2.** Square the quilt top (see Squaring, page 119).

**3.** Add the borders (see Borders, page 58). I created mitered borders.

**4.** Sandwich the quilt (see Steps for Sandwiching, page 63).

**5.** Add a label (see Labels, page 62).

**6.** Quilt your design (see Quilting, page 63) by following or echoing the motifs with matching threads. (I used an Invisi-Fil bobbin thread that matched the backing on my fabric.)

**7.** Block the quilt (see Blocking Your Quilt, page 117), and then square the quilt again.

**8.** Finish the edge (see Binding or Facing?, page 120), and then add a sleeve.

# *7 Little Abstract Flowers*

## Quiltmaker Profile and Quilt Inspiration

Heidi says, "I truly believe that I pour my heartfelt feelings into my artwork, and I pack a lot of emotion into each of my art pieces." She also says she has "…this crazy innovative side," that speaks to her now and then. Knowing that Heidi spent over a year developing her distinctive process of mosaic quilting using a digital cutter, her quilts reflect her knowledge in photography, design, editing software, quilting, and fabric values. How she has combined all these techniques to create her designs results in art quilts that are emotionally stirring and visually stunning.

Heidi's quilt *7 Little Abstract Flowers* is an excellent example of a close-up scene in nature and she says, "In 2018 I started venturing off into a possible series of abstract mosaic quilts. It was sort of the turning point in my creative road where I really just wanted not so much realism which I was already known for."

"Creating abstract quilts opened the door for me to fall in love with my newest series that I started in 2019 of non-realistic quilts, called Moroccan Mosaic quilts, and I am on fire with this style right now." Her abstract quilt *7 Little Abstract Flowers* was based on a photograph Heidi took of some ground flowers, and it was featured at the Janome Institute in Atlanta, Georgia, in August 2019. Her nonfigurative Moroccan Mosaic-style quilts are influenced by Heidi's interest in various forms of ancient and modern tile art.

Heidi has done several online interviews and her quilts have appeared in several magazines.

*Heidi Proffetty, Bridgewater, Massachusetts, 40" × 28", 2019*

Photo by Heidi Proffetty

# Mt. Rainier

*Joyce R. Becker, Kent, Washington, 19" × 15", 2020*

## Inspiration and Description

Mt. Rainier, in all its glory, will probably continue to be an inspiration to me all my life. Dan Neil's photograph of Mt. Rainier is particularly captivating because it has the lovely red foliage signaling that it is fall.

If you are new to landscape quilting, having a photograph enlarged and printed digitally is a wonderful option. With this particular design, I opted to just outline quilt it with Madeira Monofil Clear and Smoke threads, which makes it an easy quilt to accomplish. All you really need is a good-quality digital photograph to create your own digitally printed fabric. Opt to have your photograph printed on the organic cotton sateen fabric and once it is sent back to you and you sandwich and quilt it, you end up with a lovely quilt.

I also used this quilt as a sample of how to put a facing on a quilt (see Facing, page 121). You have the option of facing your quilt, adding borders, or just binding. See the steps in Fine Finishing (page 117).

Several digital printing companies print on fabric. The photo formats they prefer typically include TIF, JPG, PNG, and GIF files. Each company will lead you through the process of uploading a photograph and selecting your fabric. You will have to pay to have your photo enlarged and printed and shipped back to you.

## Materials and Supplies

*Yardage is based on 40″ of usable fabric width unless otherwise noted.*

***Enlarged photo on fabric:*** Up to 36″ × 36″

***Dark green speckled cotton:*** 1 yard for backing and facing

 Batik fabrics aren't the best for this particular method as they are too stiff.

***Threads:***
Monofilament threads: transparent and dark gray (I used 60-weight Madeira Monofil Clear and Smoke.)

Matching bobbin thread (I used InvisaFil.)

## Cutting

***Top facing and sleeve:*** Cut 3 strips 3″ × width of fabric and 1 strip 5″ × width of fabric.

## Construction

**1.** Once your printed fabric is returned to you, you may have to trim off some areas that are not part of the main photo. Square the printed image (see Squaring, page 119).

**2.** Sandwich the quilt (see Steps for Sandwiching, page 63).

**3.** Create a label for the quilt (see Labels, page 62) and position it into place.

**4.** Quilt, outlining each element in your quilt using the transparent or dark gray monofilament thread and the matching bobbin thread. (I did not block this quilt because of the printing method.)

### Fine Finishing

Add the facing and sleeve (see Binding or Facing?, page 120).

## Chapter Nine
# Creating Tantalizing Fabric

## *Moonlight Sailing*

### Quiltmaker Profile and Quilt Inspiration

Having long admired the artistry of Annette Kennedy, I crossed my fingers when I asked if she would consider contributing some of her landscape quilts for publication in this book. Much to my delight, she said yes. Asking her what makes her art unique, she responded with, "Besides making a visually beautiful scene, one of my main goals is to create visual depth in each piece. Careful fabric choices are important to get the base values and intensities right, but then applying paint in a controlled technique to the surface of the quilt is what really brings my quilts to life and makes them stand out." When you study Annette's quilts, her spark of creativity and addition of visual depth is quite apparent.

Living in Longmont, Colorado, Annette had easy access to outdoor adventures. She loves to take photographs during hikes, and she uses those photographs for the inspiration for her landscape quilts. When she first began making landscape quilts, Annette said she tried the turned-edge appliqué technique, adding, "That didn't last too long, as it was too time-consuming and didn't allow for the small detailed shapes." Her current techniques include raw-edge appliqué coupled with fusing.

While biking around Lake Dillon in Breckenridge, Colorado, one evening, Annette and her husband spotted a sailboat out in the water. They stopped to watch it move around the glistening water, resulting in a photograph of that scene which later became the inspiration for this quilt.

*Annette Kennedy, Longmont, Colorado, 13¼" × 18¼", 2019*

Photo by Van Gogh Again

Although Annette doesn't have an art degree, she says, "I have always had a creative bent and I have done many kinds of needle arts, including creating traditional quilts." When she moved to Colorado, however, she was exposed to art quilts and basically left traditional quilting in the dust.

# Aloha Spirit

*Joyce R. Becker, Kent, Washington, 33″ × 38″, 2020*

## Inspiration and Description

Creating this design calmed me down during a stressful situation in my life. It was fun to paint the fabrics using translucent textile paints outside our home on our back patio with the sun shining on my face and a slight breeze whispering through the trees.

If you have never tried painting with textile paints on fabric, it is great fun. Chapter Six (page 82) gives you lots of information related to painting with textile paints, so read those recommendations before you begin this project. As I mentioned in that chapter, I prefer painting on cotton sateen fabric (see Supplies and Resources, page 124). This fabric is 45″ wide and you don't need to wash it before you paint on it. Find a sheltered spot outside for painting if the weather is nice or a garage if it is cold or windy

## Materials and Supplies

*Yardage is based on 40" of usable fabric width unless otherwise noted.*

*Muslin (bleached or not):* 1⅜ yards

*Interfacing:* Fusible sheer or featherweight (20" width of fabric), 2½ yards

*White cotton sateen:* 2 yards (This allows ½ yard each for the sky, water, sand, and painting samples.)

*Palm tree print:* ¾ yard, with the print in a size to match the scale of your scene

> **Tip** The original palm tree fabric is primarily green shades, but colors were changed with Prismacolor artist pencils.

Appropriate palm tree fabric.

*Sailboat print:* ¼ yard

*Large-scale tropical orchid print:* ½ yard for flowers on bottom left of quilt

*Backing and sleeve:* 1½ yards

*Binding:* ½ yard

*Thin batting:* 1⅛ yards (I used Hobbs Thermore Batting.)

*Threads:*

Monofilament thread: transparent (I used 60-weight Madeira Monofil Clear.)

Matching threads for water, sky, and sand

Matching cotton thread for palm tree fronds (I used 30-weight Sulky Blendables cotton.)

Cotton thread: White, 2 spools (I used 12-weight Sulky cotton.)

Matching bobbin threads for quilting (I used InvisaFil.)

Cotton thread: White, 2 spools for bobbin (I used 50-weight Sulky cotton.)

*Embroidery hoop:* 10" diameter

*Wash-away stabilizer:* AquaMesh WashAway (by OESD)

*Repositionable spray adhesive:* I used 505 Temporary Adhesive for Fabric (by Odif)

*Spray starch*

*Prismacolor artist pencils:* Variety of colors, matching photograph of quilt

*Fabrico marking pen:* Navy blue

*Textile paint:* 1 bottle each of turquoise for water, sapphire blue for sky, white for sand, and colorless extender (I used Pebeo Setacolor or Jacquard translucent textile paint.)

*Squeeze bottles:* For mixing paint with extender

*Paint palette:* Or use disposable plastic plates or a piece of glass from a photo frame.

*Foam brushes*

*Plastic drop cloth:* Or use vinyl sheeting.

*Paperweights:* To hold down painted fabric while it dries (if you paint outdoors)

*Surgical gloves:* For painting

> **Tip** Surgical gloves from a big box store work well and you can toss them away after each use.

## Cutting

*Cotton sateen:* Cut 4 rectangles 18" × width of fabric.

*Backing:* Cut 1 rectangle 37" × 42".

*Binding:* Cut 4 strips 2½" × width of fabric.

*Sleeve:* Cut 1 strip 8½" × width of quilt plus 2".

*Thin batting:* Cut 1 rectangle 37" × 42".

## Prepare the Fabric

**1.** Make a 37″ × 42″ stabilized canvas with the muslin and interfacing. (Refer to Creating a Stabilized Canvas, page 15.)

**2.** Starch all the fabrics except the sky, backing, sleeve, and binding. (Refer to Irons and Starch, page 9.)

## Construction

*Tip* I don't recommend painting fabric inside your home. Regardless of how hard you try the textile paint will end up somewhere you don't want it to be. Wear old clothes and make sure you wear gloves. Do not paint outside if it is cold or windy.

**1.** Set up a table outside in a protected area or in the garage. Spread a plastic tarp or plastic vinyl sheeting on top of your table and anchor it with clips if it is even slightly windy.

**2.** Put on your gloves and place the turquoise paint into one of the plastic bottles or on a palette or a disposable plastic plate. Instead of water, add the colorless extender to your paint and mix well. The extender increases the transparency without affecting the viscosity of the paint and it makes it easier to distribute the paint on the cloth.

*Tip* I normally mix the paint and the extender on a palette, a piece of glass, or a plastic paper plate because I want the paint to be smooth with no defects. If you want more of a pastel translucent color, add more extender or water. Start with one part paint and one part extender. Mix well with a palette knife or plastic knife.

**3.** Now is the time to do a color test. Using a medium-size foam brush, paint a small amount of the turquoise paint on the rectangle of cotton sateen fabric that will be used for samples.

*Tip* If you want to see your painting results right away, use a blow dryer to dry the test piece of fabric. If the fabric is too dark and you want more of a pastel effect, add more extender or water to your palette.

**4.** Paint the water piece of cotton sateen. When painting large areas of fabric, like the water and sky, use a medium-size foam brush and work quickly. You don't need to saturate the entire foam brush as there is more paint on the brush than you realize. Paint quickly before the paint dries up. Try your best not to have streaks in the areas you have painted.

*Tip* You can always just mix a small amount of paint and extender and try your hand at painting a small sample first just to get the feel of the thickness of the paint and how to apply it smoothly with the foam brush.

**5.** Leave the painted cloth in place until it dries.

**6.** Once the paint is dry, heat-set it from the back of the fabric with a dry iron set on medium-high.

*Tip* Once, I forgot to heat-set a piece of fabric that I painted, and I put the painted fabric into a quilt. Unfortunately, when I blocked my quilt, the painted area of the quilt ran. Always heat-set all your coloring mediums!

**7.** Next, repeat Steps 3–6 to paint the sky and the sand pieces. I wanted the sand to be brighter than the original white color of the fabric so that's why I painted it too. The paint also kept the water fabric from bleeding through the sand fabric.

**8.** Select a suitable palm tree from the palm tree fabric, but don't cut it out. It is easier to color elements before you cut them out of the fabric. Cut a larger area around the palm tree and starch the fabric heavily.

**9.** Using the photograph as a guide, start coloring the palm fronds with the Prismacolor artist pencils. Once you have colored it as pictured, heat-set the fabric and cut out the palm tree.

**10.** Place your stabilized canvas on your working wall.

**11.** Glue and position the sky fabric into place.

*Tip* It is impossible to glue the larger fabrics in a regular gluing box. My suggestion is to lay a piece of plastic sheeting over a large table and then lay the painted fabric facedown and apply the repositionable spray adhesive. It is easier if you have a helper when you position the fabric into place on the canvas. Remember that the fabric is repositionable so you can always lift areas that are not positioned correctly.

**12.** Glue and position the water fabric into place, making sure it is level.

**13.** Using the photograph as your guide, cut the sand fabric, glue, and position into place.

**14.** Machine appliqué the sand fabric to the water fabric using a matching turquoise thread and a straight or small zigzag stitch.

**15.** Color a thin line on the top water line using the navy blue Fabrico marker.

**16.** Cut out a starched sailboat from the commercial fabric approximately the same scale as pictured. Glue and position into place.

**17.** Glue and position the palm tree into place.

**18.** Create the needle lace for the waves as described in Needle Lace or Seafoam (page 39). It may be necessary to create more than one hoop full of needle lace for this design.

**19.** Cut the needle lace into half-moon shapes for the water and glue and position into place as pictured.

**20.** Cut the waves on the shore from the needle lace suggesting foamy water and glue and position into place.

**21.** Cut out the starched orchid fabric flowers and stalks except for the 2 stalks extending off the design, glue, and position into place.

**22.** For the 2 flower stalks extending off the design, glue a piece of the backing fabric onto the backs of the flower stalks before cutting them out. Once they are cut, apply glue only to the base and position into place, to allow for the binding. Or you may add them after the binding is attached.

**23.** Baste the design with the transparent monofilament thread.

## Fine Finishing

**1.** Press the quilt top from the back (see Press Your Quilt Top, page 58).

**2.** Square the quilt top (see Squaring, page 119).

**3.** Sandwich the quilt (see Steps for Sandwiching, page 63).

**4.** Create a label for the quilt (see Labels, page 62) and position it into place.

**5.** Finish the quilting (see Quilting, page 63), block the quilt (see Blocking Your Quilt, page 117), and then square the quilt again.

**6.** Finish the edge (see Binding or Facing?, page 120), and then add a sleeve.

# *Winter Song*

## Quiltmaker Profile and Quilt Inspiration

This is one of my favorite quilts by Annette. This quilt was inspired by a trip that Annette took to Rocky Mountain National Park in the fall. Sharing that fall is her favorite season, Annette enjoyed taking photographs of the aspen trees, especially the tree trunks and the shady areas with the snow. Having never made a quilt with snow on it before, Annette managed to capture the feel of the frosty landscape, keeping her mantra for creating a piece that "…has overall visual balance, beauty, depth, and is compelling."

Speaking of detail, Annette created the controlled painting techniques that she uses on her quilts when she learned the principles of creating visual depth many years ago. Her methods of accomplishing color and value blending with paint, creating dark shadows, and adding light highlights in just the right places makes the visual dimension in this quilt, and all her quilts, pop.

Annette is fortunate to have a large basement studio that includes a storage room filled with shelving, a fabric studio, a wet studio, a full kitchen, and a bathroom, and

*Annette Kennedy, Longmont, Colorado, 25¼" × 32¼", 2020*

Photo by Van Gogh Again

she readily admits, "I am so fortunate to have this dedicated studio space." Although she has retired from teaching, she puts her studio to good use continuing to create quilts and other art, acknowledging that, "I sell my work, and landscape quilts sell well for me."

Annette says she has a set of techniques that work very well for her. The challenge she has when creating each quilt "…is to improve my ability to see things in the scene I am working from and to get better at incorporating those details that I feel are important for the piece." One of her main goals is to create a compelling piece that has overall visual balance, beauty, and depth.

# Knock Knock

## Quiltmaker Profile and Quilt Inspiration

Saying that her work is "…inspired by nature and reflects what I have seen over my life-long journey," Nanette's education and background in wildlife biology are reflected in the quilts she creates. In particular, *Knock Knock* was inspired by the research Nanette did studying the over-wintering songbirds in the bottomland hardwoods (swamps) of Eastern North Carolina. Holding a master's degree in wildlife biology, Nanette focused on the ivory-billed woodpecker, which has been listed as extinct.

As far as unique techniques go, Nanette creates many of her elements using Prismacolor pencils for shading and bridal illusion tulle. In this quilt, she specifically shaded the trees and the swampy water with the Prismacolor pencils, adding that, "When coastal rivers overflow, the water floods into the adjacent, lower-level swamp lands." The water lines on the trees, which she created using tulle, represent the water levels in the swamp over time.

For this quilt, Nanette used raw-edge appliqué to create the basic fabric design and she freehand drew the tree shapes on paper. Since the ivory-billed woodpecker

*Nanette S. Zeller, Southern Pines, North Carolina, 31" × 42", 2016*
Photo by Nanette S. Zeller

is extinct, Nanette used scientific references and rendered a digital drawing to use as a pattern. She shaded the trees and water with the Prismacolor pencils, added the shimmer on the water with layers of bridal illusion tulle, and thread painted the bird. For extra foliage on the tree tops, Nanette used a confetti technique.

Nanette and I first met when she acted as the freelance technical editor for my book *Beautifully Embellished Landscape Quilts.* My book was her first real exposure to landscape quilts, and she found herself experimenting with some of the techniques she was introduced to. She later started creating pieces that reflected her love of nature and landscape quilts. Nanette says her best ideas come from traveling. "Whether it is a trip to a National Park or a stroll around my backyard, many of my ideas come to me when I see a naturescape that ignites a quilted vision."

# Mt. Rainier Reflecting in Tipsoo Lake

## Quilt Inspiration and Process

As in my other *Mt. Rainier* quilt (page 79), Mt. Rainier is a continual source of inspiration for me, regardless of which viewpoint or season.

For this particular design, I wanted to include an image of how the mountain looks reflecting in Tipsoo Lake. It's funny, some people think you have to have a large body of water for a reflection but that's not true. You can actually have a reflection in a puddle of water.

I always like to challenge myself when I am creating a new design and I certainly did that with this quilt. Chapter Five (page 39) shows you how I created the reflecting trees. I spent hours free-motion machine embroidering the trees with a thick cotton thread so that they would pop and appear dense. Chapter Seven (page 57) demonstrates how I accomplished the machine embroidery.

I hand painted the sky and water with textile paint, and once the paint was dry, I added the hues of

*Joyce R. Becker, Kent, Washington, 29″ × 34″, July 2016*

pink with a couple of colors of Caran de' Ache wax pastels. Once the coloring applications were done, I heat-set the textile paint and wax pastels. In order to get an accurate reflection of Mt. Rainier, I made the original mountain separately before applying it to the design. I copied the mountain I had made in mirror mode and printed it on white computer-ready fabric.

I enjoyed including the beautiful lupine flowers that grow abundantly near Mt. Rainier, and I also included a shoreline created with bonded Angelina. To learn about Angelina, see Chapter Six (page 52). If you ever have the opportunity to visit Mt. Rainier, you will remember it always as it definitely leaves a lasting impression.

# Victorian Landscape

## Quiltmaker Profile and Quilt Inspiration

Inspired by a visit to Victoria in British Columbia, Canada, at sunset, and based on a photograph she took, Lenore's *Victorian Landscape* quilt is filled with a riot of colorful flowers, textures, and shading that makes it come alive. The calming waters and reflections at sunset with the backdrop of the mountains and sweeping trees makes this a place anyone would want to visit.

I have admired Lenore's landscape art quilts for many years. Her specific attention to detail is what draws me into her quilts, and I suspect it's the reason she has won so many top awards at national quilt shows. Regarding her landscape quilts, Lenore says, "After trying many different ways of fusing, I came up with my own technique that allows me to create realistic art quilts using raw-edged fusing and a pattern that I make from my own photos."

Additionally, what makes Lenore's quilts different and unique is the fact that she adds very fine details and shading with fabric paints after she fuses her design. This in turn adds to the realism. Lenore is like me in that she buys fabric for her stash when she sees something she likes. As an added bonus, she also has the opportunity to go shopping in her mom's stash because her mother has four times more fabric than she does and lives very close by.

After working in the "watercolor" quilting genre (using small fabric pieces to create a sort of watercolor painting) for some time, Lenore found it too confining and went on to develop and extend her style into what she calls *impressionistic fabric blending*. The result is her very detailed art quilts. She says she enjoys making beautiful landscapes with dramatic color, texture, and warmth in a technique that uses hundreds of different fabrics cut randomly and blended into a design. (For another of Lenore's art quilts, see *Old Port Yvoire II*, page 93.)

*Lenore Crawford, Midland, Michigan, 45" × 34", 2018*

Photo by Lenore Crawford

# Fantasy Forest

## Quilt Inspiration and Process

A long time in the making, this design was in my head for years before I had the time to actually fabricate it. The incredible hand-dyed fabric by Judy Robertson that I used for the sky was actually the inspiration for this design because of the influence of the sun in the upper left corner of the fabric. Many landscape designs are created from an inspirational photograph or image but not always. This quilt proves that the fabric can also be an inspiration for a quilt.

After I saw a photo of the redwoods with the sun filtering in between the giant trees, I knew I had an idea for my design. I didn't copy the image; it just sparked my imagination to create the design.

There was a lot of trial and error with this design. I tried many different fabrics for the sunbeams before I discovered a white tulle fabric that was thicker than the regular bridal illusion tulle you might ordinarily think of using. In order to weave the sunbeams through the trees, I had to lightly glue the trees in place with repositional spray adhesive (page 8) and lift and position them one by one to insert the sunbeams.

Speaking of the trees, it turns out I only had enough fabric for the large trees in the foreground. I had to "recreate" the rest of the tree fabric by painting blended Tsukineko inks and wax pastels onto cotton sateen fabric. I find that investing in quality coloring mediums is crucial for the creation of many of my landscape quilts.

Quite by accident, I discovered the hand-dyed trim on the bottom of the quilt at a quilt show, purchased it, and discovered I had just enough of the trim to embellish the quilt.

Cutting out the heavily starched and bonded fabrics for the tree boughs seemed to take forever and boy, did I have blisters afterward. The pathway and border fabrics are from the Stonehenge collection by Linda Ludovico for Northcott Fabrics.

*Joyce R. Becker, Kent, Washington,*
*45" × 43", 2010*

# Flatirons Symphony

## Quiltmaker Profile and Quilt Inspiration

Inspired by the beautiful scenery around her, Annette says that the flatirons rock formations in Boulder, Colorado, are "...very recognizable and almost anyone who has been there would recognize these mountains immediately." I was amazed seeing the in-progress photographs of this quilt during its creation, especially the cloud formations, which are very unique. I swear, I can almost feel the rain showers coming down.

It is interesting to find out how other artists work, so when I asked Annette if she works in chaos with fabrics piled on every surface, she said, "There are days when fabric gets out of control and is everywhere. However, I can't stand that for more than a day or two before I need to get everything back in order so I can find what I am looking for." I, on the other hand, work in total chaos until I have selected all the fabrics I need for a design and have done all my cutting, gluing, and positioning of my elements onto my design.

My studio during my "creative process"
Photo by Joyce R. Becker

*Annette Kennedy, Longmont, Colorado, 28¼" × 21¾", 2018*

Photo by Van Gogh Again

# Lily Pond

## Quiltmaker Profile and Quilt Inspiration

Married to former Hawaii State Attorney General Michael A. Lily, Cindy created a series of lily-themed quilts in her husband's honor. *Lily Pond* was featured in Cindy's book *Fabric Painting with Cindy Walter* (page 125). Cindy has authored or coauthored around ten books featuring a plethora of quilting techniques.

I had the pleasure of meeting Cindy at my quilt guild, Evergreen Piecemakers in Kent, Washington, many years ago when she came to lecture for us. I owned her book *Snippet Sensations* and I created two quilts using her techniques that I brought along to share with her. As a result, she featured my quilts *Heceta Head Celebration* and *Awakening* in her book *More Snippet Sensations*.

A highly visible professional quilt artist, author, teacher, lecturer, and television host, Cindy has taught worldwide for many years, including such venues as International Quilt Festival in Houston, Texas; Sew Expo; New Zealand Quilt Symposium; Quilt Week in Yokohama, Japan; and more. She has appeared on many PBS television quilting shows including *Sew Perfect*, *Simply Quilts*, *Home Matters*, *America Sews*, and *Kay Wood's Quilting Friends*, in addition to the Discovery Channel, and *The Quilt Show* with Alex Anderson and Ricky Tims. Cindy also enjoys teaching on quilting cruises.

Cindy created *Lily Pond* by painting a colorwash with thin transparent textile paints on a white fabric. She said, "I had to work very fast to blend the colors before they dried." Once her colorful background dried, she freehand painted the water lily pads using thick opaque and metallic fabric paints. She painted the borders separately and attached them to the quilt top once the center of the quilt was finished.

Cindy says, "The sky's the limit when I am creating quilts and there are no rules," adding, "I actually dream up some of my quilts in my sleep." Cindy works in a small studio on their property in Hawaii and says, "It's not fancy, but I know that the quality of a quilter's studio doesn't determine their creativity."

*Cindy Walter, Kula, Hawaii, 63" × 56", 2006*

Photo by Diane Pedersen of C&T Publishing

# *Old Port Yvoire II*

## Quiltmaker Profile and Quilt Inspiration

Imagine having the opportunity to live on Lake Geneva (or *Lac Léman*), France, in a small village with the picturesque Alps in the distance. Lenore spent many years there and took a photograph of Old Port Yvoire when she lived there. Lenore says, "I have been greatly influenced by the French culture and architecture, and I really enjoy the lifestyle of the French."

One of Lenore's gifts when it comes to creating realistic landscape quilts is her incredible talent with architecture. Having the ability to design buildings with the correct angles using fabric that represents the authentic-appearing building materials, imparting shading, texture, and dimension all at the same time, is a true gift. An artist in every sense of the word, Lenore's award-winning art has gathered the attention of quilters worldwide and she has traveled to teach and lecture all over the United States at many prestigious venues as well as traveling to Canada, France, and beyond.

*Lenore Crawford, Midland, Michigan, 34" × 34", 2020*
Photo by Lenore Crawford

What makes Lenore's art unique and different from other artist's work is her ability to "…add the extra details to the finished pieces that make my designs nearly photo realistic."

All of us work in different ways and Lenore says, "I work in my studio in the afternoon after I have done my chores. When I finish a project, I clean up my space and I can't start another piece until my space is organized, as it keeps my mind organized too."

Lenore is fortunate to have a spacious studio in the attic of her home that has a skylight and a lounging area, and she typically only creates quilts when she is alone without distractions.

## Chapter Ten

# Utilizing Commercial Fabrics

## The Smoky Mountains

*Joyce R. Becker, Kent, Washington, 17" × 23", 2020*

## Inspiration and Description

Teaching and lecturing has given me the opportunity to meet quilters worldwide and has incredible perks. When I taught for the Western North Carolina Quilters Guild in Hendersonville, North Carolina, I fell in love with the quilters, the town, the beautiful nearby waterfalls, and the Smoky Mountains.

The Smoky Mountains are very different from the mountains I see here in Washington State. They are rounder in stature and the value and scale of the mountains increase gradually. This quilt is perfect as a study in how to create a successful perspective in landscape quilts. Can you see the subtle differences in value and scale as you come forward in the design? If you are new to the landscape quilting genre, this is an excellent choice for a beginner to try.

## Materials and Supplies

*Yardage is based on 40″ of usable fabric width unless otherwise noted.*

**Muslin (bleached or not):** ¾ yard

**Interfacing:** Fusible sheer or featherweight (20″ width of fabric), 1½ yards

**Sky print:** ½ yard
(I used Pastel from Artisan Batiks: Patina Handpaints Stripes collection by Lunn Studios for Robert Kaufman Fabrics.)

**Gray mountain print:** ¾ yard
(I used Gray fabric from Stonehenge Gradations Ombré collection by Linda Ludovico for Northcott Fabrics.)

**Green mountain print:** ¾ yard
(I used Avocado fabric from Stonehenge Gradations Ombré collection by Linda Ludovico for Northcott Fabrics.)

**Avocado/leaf green print:** ¾ yard for green mountain and second from bottom row foreground
(I used a leaf print with subtle trees cotton batik.)

**Mountain with trees print:** ¾ yard for foreground
(I used Lush Forests–Leaf green from North American Wildlife collection by Elizabeth's Studio.)

**Dark pine green tulle:** ⅓ yard for overlay over 2 rows of mountains

**Dark green netting:** ¼ yard for overlay of darkest green ombré mountain

**White tulle:** ⅓ yard (*optional*)

**Backing and sleeve:** 1 yard

**Green striped batik:** ⅜ yard for binding

**Thin batting:** 1 yard (I used Hobbs Thermore Batting.)

**Threads:**

Monofilament threads: transparent and dark gray (I used 60-weight Monofil Madeira Clear and Smoke.)

Matching threads for mountains and trees

Matching bobbin threads (I used InvisaFil.)

**Prismacolor artist pencils:** Light, medium, and dark gray

**Repositionable spray adhesive:** I used 505 Temporary Adhesive for Fabric (by Odif)

**Spray starch**

## Cutting

**Sky:** Cut 1 rectangle 18″ × 6″.

**Backing:** Cut 1 rectangle 21″ × 27″.

**Sleeve:** Cut 1 rectangle 8½″ × width of quilt plus 2″.

**Binding:** Cut 4 strips 2½″ × width of fabric.

**Batting:** Cut 1 rectangle 21″ × 27″.

# Prepare the Fabric

1. Make a 21″ × 27″ stabilized canvas with the muslin and interfacing. (Refer to Creating a Stabilized Canvas, page 15.)

2. Starch all the fabrics except the sky, backing, sleeve, and binding. (Refer to Irons and Starch, page 9.)

# Construction

1. Audition the fabrics on your design wall to make sure they look good together.

2. Glue and position the sky into place.

3. Cut the top mountain in the distance from the lightest area in the gray ombré fabric; glue and position into place.

4. Repeat for the next row of mountains but select a slightly darker portion of the gray ombré fabric; glue and position into place.

5. Select the lightest color of the green ombré fabric, cut out the next mountain, and glue and position into place.

6. Select a darker value gray for the next mountain; cut, glue, and position into place.

7. Select a darker value green ombré fabric for the next mountain, cut, glue, and position into place.

8. Select the darkest value of the green ombré fabric for the next mountain, cut, glue, and position into place.

9. Cut out the next mountain from the green batik fabric, adding small tree shapes as you cut; glue and position into place.

10. Cut, glue, and position the green tulle overlay into place extending over the darkest green ombré fabric and the green batik fabric that you cut with the small trees.

11. Cut, glue, and position the dark green netting over the darkest green ombré fabric.

12. Cut the forest fabric in the foreground as pictured in the photograph so it appears like there are trees extending into the fabric above it. Make the trees different heights to make the scene look realistic. Glue and position into place.

13. Baste the quilt top, selecting the transparent and dark gray monofilament threads according to the value of the fabric. You can baste this design using free-motion or with an embroidery foot using a regular stitch. Try to stitch as close to the edge of each element as you can.

14. Trim away the excess tulle and netting. (See Chapter Four, Basting, page 33.)

## Fine Finishing

1. Use the Prismacolor artist pencils to lightly color the top edge of the gray mountains. Use the lightest color for the furthest gray mountain in the distance and so on.

2. Use the matching threads to zigzag a narrow stitch on top of the green mountain fabric that doesn't have trees to highlight the mountains.

3. On the dark green ombré fabric, free-motion stitch small pine trees with a matching thread as pictured on the quilt.

4. On the batik fabric, use a matching thread to free-motion branches onto the trees that you cut out as pictured on the quilt.

5. Steam press the back of the quilt to remove all the wrinkles and puckers.

6. Square the quilt top (see Squaring, page 119).

7. Sandwich the quilt (see Steps for Sandwiching, page 63).

8. Create a label for the quilt (see Labels, page 62) and position it into place.

9. Finish the quilting (see Quilting, page 63), block the quilt (see Blocking Your Quilt, page 117), and then square the quilt again.

10. Finish the edge (see Binding or Facing?, page 120), and then add a sleeve.

# A Light to Guide Them Home

## Quiltmaker Profile and Quilt Inspiration

Helene's focus in art for quite some time has primarily been with fiber and quilting. As a native Californian previously living on the Monterey Peninsula, Helene showed an early interest in art and explored many different mediums.

Having grown up in a coastal town, Helene says, "I have always been drawn to the ocean. Now that I am living inland, I really miss the experience of living where you can see, smell and hear the ocean, the constant roar in the background, the cries of the seagulls, barking seals, and the mournful call of a foghorn."

Living inland in the Pacific Northwest now, Helene revels in the memories of the sea as subject matter for many of her quilts. From an early age, Helene says she had a keen interest in art and explored many different mediums. Her primary focus and passion, however, has been fiber and quilting.

*A Light to Guide Them Home* blends Helen's methods of strip piecing with needle-turn appliqué and raw-edge appliqué. She looks at her artistic process as a form of storytelling. She gets visions in her head sometimes in response to music or the written word or from a particularly beautiful scene. This quilt does not represent a real place; it was composed from Helene's imagination and from her experience living near the coast.

Admitting that she probably has the world's largest stash of landscape-suitable fabrics in her studio, she usually is able to start a new design with the fabric she has on hand. She has converted a spare bedroom into her studio and says, "It's usually a disaster area because it looks like a hoarder lives there." Followed by, "Oh wait, a hoarder does live here." She even compares her sewing room to an archaeological dig. I suspect many of us work in the same environment.

*Helene Knott, Oregon City, Oregon, 52" × 35", 2020*

Photo by David Knott

# Kitty in the Garden

## Quilt Inspiration and Process

This was a fun quilt to create and I used a variety of commercial fabrics and techniques. I didn't have anyone in particular who loves cats in mind for this quilt; it was actually inspired by several lovely landscape fabrics that I already had in my stash. I basically just started pulling fabrics and auditioning them together to see what worked and what didn't work. I spent quite a bit of time cutting out and arranging the flowers and foliage for this quilt and it was almost like I was doing a floral arrangement for my home. I thought the pathway needed something on it and I was delighted to discover a commercial fabric in my stash with kitty cats on it. It worked perfectly!

I've always liked gardens with arches that look out into the distance, so I created one in this design. The view of the water and the mountain help to build in the perspective or the feeling of distance in this design. I also enjoyed positioning two different types of large trees next to the garden wall. Although the painted fabric for the garden wall and arch

*Joyce R. Becker, Kent, Washington, 30″ × 33″, 2013*
From the collection of Janet White (my twin sister)

reads more abstract than realistic, I thought it added an extra bit of whimsy to the design as did the striped inner border fabric. The outer border, using a fabric from the Stonehenge Gradations Ombré collection by Linda Ludovico for Northcott Fabrics, enhances the design.

This is one of those quilts that I just had fun with. I didn't have a specific goal or exhibition opportunity for this quilt. Sometimes, we just need to let go, play, and make a quilt for the sheer joy of it. When my twin sister saw this quilt, she exclaimed, "It's mine," so I gifted it to her.

# Seductive Tranquility

## Quiltmaker Profile and Quilt Inspiration

*Seductive Tranquility* was inspired by the beautiful striped batik fabric in the background. Nanette says, "The colors of the batik remind me of a rich, dark, and colorful sunset," and it reminds her of moments in her life when she saw the sun behind the mountains.

For this design, Nanette added a stabilizer to the back of her quilt top so that she could accomplish her extensive thread painting to add definition to the tree and grassy knoll. She also quilted her design heavily to add accents to the mountains, sky, and water.

Nanette says her favorite part of the process of creating landscape quilts is "…the machine work. Whether it is the thread painting or free-motion quilting, I feel like I get into a zone when I do the machine work." She also added that she feels the machine work is meditative and a thought-filled process for her.

Regarding her art, Nanette says she normally just goes for it. "I get a vision and I proceed forward with only a basic plan." She says she gets stuck frequently and doesn't know what to do next but that she likes the process. Her process is to leave her work on the design wall and just let the ideas percolate. I have to agree with Nanette because as artists, we need to let our minds catch up sometimes before we proceed.

Wondering what got Nanette into quilting to begin with, she told me, "A friend of mine invited me to a quilting bee and I wasn't very interested in learning; however, I was looking to meet some new people and make friends." She asked her friend if it was okay if she went along and just knitted and her friend said yes. "Before I knew it, I was piecing blocks and buying lots of fabric, and the rest is history."

*Nanette S. Zeller, Southern Pines, North Carolina, 16" × 29", 2014*
Photo by Nanette S. Zeller

# Quaking Aspens—Summer

## Quilt Inspiration and Process

On a road trip to Boulder, Colorado, to tape *The Quilt Show* with Alex Anderson and Ricky Tims, my husband and I extended our trip and drove to Grand Junction, Colorado, to visit my stepson, Mike Simmons, and his wife, Charlene. (Mike is a talented photographer and videographer, and he photographed all the instructional photographs for this book.)

When we visited them, they drove us up onto a nearby mesa so we could witness the beauty firsthand. One of the things I always dreamed of seeing in Colorado were the quaking aspen trees blowing in the wind. The aspen trees were a sight to behold, and since it was summer, the green leaves looked like they were actually quaking or trembling in the wind. I created this summer version of *Quaking Aspens* as a Christmas gift for Mike and Charlene. This memory inspired me to create the entire series. (The three quilts in this series use the techniques I describe in my book *Quick Little Landscape Quilts*.)

Instead of creating a canvas and a wall quilt, the quilts in this series are created on fast2fuse Heavy Interfacing (by C&T Publishing) and matted and framed.

*Joyce R. Becker, Kent, Washington, 17" × 14", 2011*
From the collection of Mike and Charlene Simmons
Photo by Michael R. Simmons

# *Quaking Aspens—Fall*

*Joyce R. Becker, Kent, Washington, 20″ × 16″, 2020*

This quilt has a photo mat but not a frame.

# Quaking Aspens—Winter

*Joyce R. Becker, Kent, Washington, 17" × 14" (includes frame), 2020*

## Inspiration and Description

As I mentioned earlier, I was inspired to do this series by the beautiful quaking aspen trees in Colorado. Even in the stark, bitter cold of winter, the aspen trees steal the scene with their recognizable markings. Although I used a commercial aspen tree fabric, adding enhancements with wax pastels, a black fine-tip permanent marker, and zigzag stitching with a monofilament thread on the trunks brought the trees to life.

## Materials and Supplies

*Yardage is based on 40″ of usable fabric width unless otherwise noted.*

*Sky print:* ½ yard
(I used Snow sky from Winter Companions collection by Abraham Hunter for Elizabeth's Studio.)

*Snowy pine tree print:* ½ yard
(I used Snowy Trees from Landscape Medley collection by Elizabeth's Studio.)

*Mottled gray:* ⅓ yard for snowy mountain fabric in background

*Quaking aspen or birch tree print:* ¾ yard (Look for correct scale and gray tones.)

*Heavy interfacing:* 17″ × 14″ (I used fast2fuse Heavy Interfacing by C&T Publishing.)

*White batting:* ½ yard for snow

*Thread:*

Monofilament thread: transparent
(I used 60-weight Madeira Monofil Clear.)

Cotton thread: Light to medium gray
(I used 12-weight Sulky cotton.)

Matching bobbin threads (I used InvisaFil.)

*Picture frame:* 17″ × 14″

*Wax pastels:* Light gray, dark gray, and light blue
(I used Caran d'Ache Neocolor II Water Soluble Wax Pastels.)

*Acrylic ink:* White
(I used Liquitex Professional Acrylic Ink.)

*Black fine-tip permanent marker*

*Sea sponge*

*Paint palette:* Or use a heavy-duty paper plate or glass from a photo frame.

*Nonstick pressing sheets*

*Repositionable spray adhesive:* I used 505 Temporary Adhesive for Fabric (by Odif)

*Cardboard box:* For gluing, about 8″ × 10″ with 1″–2″ sides

*Spray starch*

## Cutting

*Sky fabric:* Cut 1 rectangle 14″ × 11″.

*Heavy interfacing:* Cut 1 rectangle 14″ × 11″.

## Prepare the Fabric

**1.** Starch all the fabrics except the sky. (Refer to Irons and Starch, page 9.)

**2.** Cut the mountain and pine trees.

**3.** Cut out individual quaking aspen trees. Cut some of the aspen trees smaller to create the correct scale of medium-size trees and smaller trees in the distance.

## Construction

**1.** Fuse the sky fabric to the heavy interfacing.

*Tip* **Use a nonstick pressing sheet above and below the heavy interfacing to prevent the glue from sticking to your iron.**

**2.** Glue and position the mountain and pine trees into place.

**3.** Position the batting below the mountain and the pine trees and fuse into place.

**4.** Baste the sky, mountain, and pine trees into place with the transparent monofilament thread.

**5.** Quilt the snow as pictured in the photograph. Note that the aspen trees have not been positioned into the design yet.

**6.** Add shadows in the snow with the light blue wax pastel using a light touch.

**7.** Sponge the snow or batting with the white Liquitex ink to add the effect of snowflakes. Let the ink dry and heat-set it with a pressing cloth.

**8.** Start with the smallest aspen trees in the distance and glue and position into place, followed by the medium aspen trees and then the large aspen trees. Make sure all the trees extend all the way to the top of the design.

### Fine Finishing

**1.** Baste the aspen trees into place using transparent monofilament thread and a large zigzag stitch with an open-toe appliqué foot and the feed dogs up. Extend the width of the stitch so it covers the width of each tree. A zigzag stitch with the monofilament thread adds to the realism of how the bark looks.

**2.** Color the trees with the light gray wax pastel using a light touch.

**3.** Color the right side of each of the trees with the dark gray wax pastel with a stronger touch, implicating that the right side of the trees are in the shade as pictured in the photograph. Move the wax pastel in a small zigzag motion when applying the color.

**4.** Use the fine-tip black Sharpie to add the markings to the aspen trees.

**5.** Heat-set the coloring applications using a nonstick pressing sheet above and below the quilt.

**6.** Add free-motion limbs and branches to the aspen trees using the gray thread.

**7.** Use the back side of the frame board to measure what size you should trim your design to be. The frame back in my design measured 11″ × 14″.

**8.** Remove the glass from the frame and slip the design into the frame and cover it with the frame back.

# Night Glow in Hawaii

## Quilt Inspiration and Process

I was inspired to create *Night Glow in Hawaii* after seeing the remarkable art of James Coleman. Although James is famous for his work with Disney, his Hawaii-themed landscape paintings depict mostly moonlight versions of what the islands looked like without the hustle and bustle of tourists. His amazing ability to translate emotion into his work seems to romanticize his scenes and make you wish you could stay there forever.

Having been to Hawaii once a year for the past twenty years or so, I always make a beeline to the fabric stores that carry Hawaiian-themed fabrics when I arrive. Consequently, I was prepared with several different flora and fauna fabrics in my stash for this quilt. The most difficult part of the design was the waterfall area placed between the two mountains. I ended up painting the large waterfall with textile paints and placed overlays of batting on top of the painted areas to make it look realistic. Once the main waterfall was complete, I enjoyed placing foliage and palm trees over the edges of the mountains to make the design more interesting.

*Joyce R. Becker, Kent, Washington, 25" × 27", 2020*

Once you get away from the cities and towns in the Hawaiian Islands, the stars are abundant, so I added them to the sky using Swarovski crystals. I also included an overlay of dark navy tulle on the quilt top, except for the sky, to make the scene more dreamlike and to have the elements meld together. I added a dark navy trim to the borders to set off the design. This quilt is also an example of a border added to a quilt that originally didn't have one (see Adding a Border to an Already-Quilted Quilt, page 42).

# Hidden Cove 3

## Quiltmaker Profile and Quilt Inspiration

The saying, "Still waters run deep," to me describes Helene's philosophy about art. Helene believes that "…art is our universal language, and it is a unique characteristic of human nature to create visuals that go beyond function into abstract thought."

In her landscape quilts, Helene likes to think poetically and tries to capture more than just the visual imagery. She wants the experience of being in nature to involve all your senses, not just the sight or what you are viewing. If you are looking at one of her seascape quilts, for example, she wants you to "…hear the whispering as the waves caress the beach, to hear the plaintive cries of the seagulls off in the distance, and to smell the salt air and the seaweed."

Helene says that she really enjoys the challenge of finding just the right fabrics to incorporate into her quilts and that her favorite part of quilt making is the designing aspect. Stating that she has made lots of other kinds of quilts—including traditional, innovative, contemporary, abstract, and quilts inspired by ancient art forms—she keeps returning to her favorite, landscape quilts.

The quilt *Hidden Cove 3* reflects Helene's memories of exploring the rugged landscapes of Big Sur and Northern California

*Helene Knott, Oregon City, Oregon, 17" × 24", 2013*

Photo by David Knott

and similar landscapes on the rocky coast of Oregon. "The idyllic beaches I have been to are often revealed behind layers of cliffs and rocks creating a beautiful opportunity to pull landscape elements out into the borders of the quilt to make a multi-layered scene that echoes the experience of coming upon these unexpected gems."

Helene incorporated both needle-turn appliqué and raw-edge appliqué in this quilt. Adding four borders to her design gave her the opportunity to extend the elements of the quilt into the border, adding visual interest.

# A Winter's Night

## Quilt Inspiration and Process

*A Winter's Night* is the result of an inspiring Japanese fabric that kept calling me until I caved in and bought it. Wandering through the vendors during my lunch break when teaching at the International Quilt Festival in Houston, Texas, I spotted the tree fabric that was the basis for this quilt. I fondled the fabric, held it up, and then I looked at the price tag and said to myself, "Do I really *need* this fabric?" I left without it and went back to teach. For some reason, this fabric just wouldn't leave me alone and it kept hounding me, so I marched back to the vendor the next day and bought a yard.

The fabric, as printed, didn't exactly work in my design, so I had to manipulate it. I ended up cutting several extra trees to set on a snowy bank, which helped build in the correct perspective. I also hid a wolf in the forest just for fun. Do you see it?

*Joyce R. Becker, Kent, Washington, 33" × 29", 2019*

To me, this quilt evokes a feeling or mood of a brisk, dark winter night with a forbidding frostbitten ocean and an icy, remote shoreline surrounded by trees. The fabric itself gives the appearance of a light shining through the trees like moonlight.

Since I wanted to make this quilt a frosty night scene, one of the fabrics from the Stonehenge Gradations Ombré collection by Linda Ludovico for Northcott Fabrics was perfect for the sky and the water and added visual interest with its dark swirling motion. The sky seemed to beg for tiny twinkling stars, so I fused Swarovski crystals into the sky to make it come alive and make the quilt a bit more interesting. I selected rocks to line the shoreline of the quilt that were the correct scale and color and shaded them with a black fine-tip permanent marker and wax pastels. I quilted the sky and water using a free-motion very small stipple stitch.

I also listened to the "quilt whisperer" in my dreams, who told me that this quilt needed no borders or binding to frame it. Consequently, I created a facing for it (see Facing, page 121). I wonder if I am the only one who listens to their dreams when they design quilts. . . .

# Sequoia Kings

## Quiltmaker Profile and Quilt Inspiration

Inspired by the towering *Sequoia sempervirens*, commonly known as the coast redwood trees of Northern California, Nanette fondly remembers a visit to the Muir Woods National Monument where she was "…filled with a sense of spirituality that I believe only a 1,200-year-old tree could provide." Her quilt celebrates her love and fascination with the magical redwood trees.

Using an enlargement of a simple pen-and-ink sketch that she executed, Nanette created appliqué pattern pieces. As a quilter who doesn't draw well, I am jealous of landscape quilt artists who have the ability to draw out their quilts and use their drawings to make their own templates. Nanette added extensive texture and dimension by thread painting the tree trunks and foliage and densely quilting to enhance the landscape and the sky.

*Nanette S. Zeller, Southern Pines, North Carolina, 18″ × 18″, 2020*

Photo by Nanette S. Zeller

Given her prior occupation as a wildlife biologist, Nanette draws on her experience and knowledge of nature to create nature-inspired innovative mixed-media textile art. An award-winning art quilter, Nanette has appeared on *Quilting Arts TV* and her work has appeared in quilting and textile publications including *Quilting Arts* magazine. She is also the two-time award recipient of the Regional Artist Grant Project through the Arts Council of Fayetteville, North Carolina.

Asked if she has invented any particular techniques, Nanette says her "Painted Quilt Canvas" is unique to her. Nanette says when she uses this technique that "…I treat my fabric as a traditional art painter would. I prep the quilted surfaces with primers and paints that are typically used for stretched canvases, resulting in a stiff quilted canvas that really shows the quilting designs." Nanette says she stores her quilts "…by rolling them on muslin-covered pool noodles that I have cut to size, and then I put them in a narrow, cloth bag which is made to fit each particular quilt."

# Paradise

*Joyce R. Becker, Kent, Washington, 16½" × 14" (outside frame measurement), 2017*

## Inspiration and Description

Here's another quilt made using the techniques in my book *Quick Little Landscape Quilts*, where the quilts are built on heavy interfacing and matted and framed. These quilts are quick and easy and make such wonderful gifts for family and friends. They are also fun to make with a group of quilting friends or as a workshop for quilting guilds where you can share fabric and ideas. In my online workshop through C&T's Creative Spark Online Learning platform (page 127), I teach how to design and construct this type of quilt, because creating one is much easier in scope than designing a regular landscape quilt. Designing them also gives you instant gratification, and you can actually finish crafting one or two in just a day. I originally got started making this type of quilt for Christmas gifts for friends and family. I then figured they were so much fun to make, why not write another how-to quilting book?

## Materials and Supplies

*Yardage is based on 40″ of usable fabric width unless otherwise noted.*

*Tip* You can make your interfacing and design a little bit larger if you want and slide it around in the photo mat to see which portion you like best after the design is finished.

**Light turquoise with clouds:** ⅛ yard for sky
(You can hand dye or hand paint clouds on fabric, if you wish.)

**Medium to medium-dark turquoise:** ⅛ yard for ocean

**Sand print (without yellow undertones):** ⅛ yard
(Consider both sides of the fabric. The *wrong side* of my sand fabric was perfect; the right side was too dark.)

**White 100% cotton muslin:** ⅛ yard for sand lining

**Speckled blue and white:** ½ yard for waves

**Palm tree print:** 4″ × 8″

**Sailboat print:** 2″ × 4″

**Heavy fusible interfacing:** 14″ × 12″ (I used fast2fuse Heavy Interfacing by C&T Publishing.)

**Photo mat:** 14″ × 12″

**Picture frame:** 16½″ × 14″

**Large, sturdy paper plate**

**Pencil**

**Nonstick pressing sheets:** 2

**Repositional spray adhesive:** I used 505 Temporary Adhesive for Fabric Spray (by Odif).

**Fabric glues (2):** Fabric glue pen or Roxanne Glue-Baste-It; Elmer's School Glue

**Threads:**

Monofilament thread: transparent
(I used 60-weight Madeira Monofil Clear.)

Matching quilting threads for sky, ocean, sand, and waves

Cotton thread for palm tree
(I used 30-weight Sulky Blendables cotton.)

Matching bobbin threads (I used InvisaFil.)

Cotton thread (1 or 2 spools) for top and bobbin to create needle lace
(I used 12-weight Sulky cotton.)

**Embroidery hoop:** 10″ diameter

**Wash-away stabilizer:** AquaMesh WashAway (by OESD)

**Spray starch**

*Tip* If you find a good commercial sailboat fabric with motifs that are too large or too small, remember you can reduce or enlarge a boat image from the fabric on your printer and print the resized image on computer-ready fabric. Or you can create your own sailboat with fabric you have on hand.

## Cutting

**Starched sky, ocean, sand, and lining:** Cut 1 rectangle 4½″ × 14″ from each.
(Note: Double-check to make sure the ocean fabric has a level top edge; you don't want a wonky ocean.)

# Prepare the Fabric

Starch all the fabrics except the sky. (Refer to Irons and Starch, page 9.)

# Construction

**1.** Using the spray adhesive, glue the muslin fabric to whichever side of the sand fabric you do not want to show in your quilt.

**2.** Position the sky and ocean fabrics on top of the heavy fusible interfacing.

**3.** Make sure the top portion of the ocean fabric lays on top of the sky fabric. If you position it the other way, you will see the darker ocean fabric bleeding under the sky fabric.

**4.** Place the interfaced sand fabric on top of the water fabric.

**5.** Use a large paper plate as a template to draw a curve on the sand fabric with a pencil. Refer to the quilt photo (page 109) to get the right angle. Make sure you don't make the curve too deep or there will be no ocean fabric underneath.

Line the sand fabric so the water fabric doesn't bleed through.

**6.** Place a nonstick pressing sheet underneath and on top of the sandwich of the interfacing and fabrics.

**7.** Press with a medium-hot iron with *no steam* until the fabrics are fused to the interfacing.

 **Wait a few minutes for the nonstick pressing sheets to cool before touching them, otherwise you may burn yourself.**

**8.** When cool, test to see if the fabrics are fused to the interfacing.

**9.** Glue the top edges of the fabrics that are overlapped (the top portions of the ocean and sand). Use a glue pen or Roxanne Glue-Baste-It.

**10.** Let the glue dry.

**11.** Place microtex #60 needle in your sewing machine for basting the elements.

**12.** Using the transparent monofilament thread on the top and in the bobbin of your sewing machine, stitch around the perimeter of the design as close to the edges as you can.

**13.** Stitch the top ocean line and top sand line as close to the edges as you can.

 **If the fabric easily frays, do a zigzag stitch versus a straight stitch on your sewing machine.**

**14.** Change your needle to a topstitch #90 needle for the free-motion quiting. Free-motion machine quilt the sky using a white thread, following the patterns in the fabric that resemble clouds.

**15.** Free-motion machine quilt the ocean with a matching or a blendable-type thread in a pleasing fashion that looks like ocean water gently rippling.

**16.** Free-motion machine quilt the sand with a matching thread in a small stipple fashion.

**17.** Referring to the sample, cut 10 wave shapes similar to half-moon shapes from the heavily starched speckled fabric. They should measure approximately 1½″ wide by 2″–3″ long. Make sure your wave shapes have dips on the top and bottom so no two look alike.

**18.** Referring to the quilt photo (page 109), position the speckled wave shapes on the curve of the sand shoreline until you have an interesting configuration.

**19.** Glue the waves together on the back side of the fabric using a glue pen or Roxanne Glue-Baste-It.

**20.** Position the glued waves into place.

**21.** Baste the waves in place using the transparent monofilament thread, going around the perimeter of each wave shape.

**22.** Create "seafoam" in the embroidery hoop filled with the wash-away stabilizer. Use the white 12-weight cotton thread in the top and in the bobbin and an embroidery or topstitch #90 needle. Place the embroidery hoop with the stabilizer under the needle. Begin stitching long lines close together in little circles, building up the thread to create the foam going one direction. Come back and stitch in the other direction doing the same thing, filling in the spaces. Stitch quickly or your thread might hang up and break.

*Tip* All the threads need to be connected together. Leave fairly small holes versus larger holes or you will end up with a long string of thread instead of seafoam when you wash away the stabilizer.

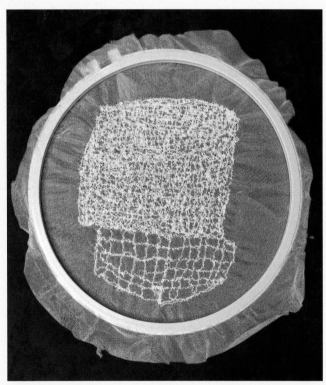

To create seafoam in a hoop with wash-away stabilizer, stitch a grid then fill it in.

**23.** Once you have a hoop full of seafoam take the stabilizer out of the hoop and let it soak in warm water for a few minutes to dissolve. Once the stabilizer is dissolved, rinse the seafoam with warm water to make sure all the residue is gone.

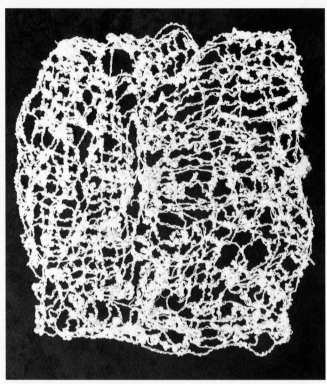

Seafoam after it is rinsed and dried

**24.** Place the seafoam on a towel and let it dry overnight. If you are in a hurry, you can blow dry the seafoam with a hair dryer.

**25.** Visually divide the seafoam into thirds widthwise and cut it apart. Try to avoid having strings hanging down by clipping near intersections.

**26.** Audition the cut seafoam next to the waves until you have it in a configuration you like.

**27.** Lightly spray the back of each piece of seafoam with the temporary adhesive and position and mold it into place until you have all of it adhered just beneath the specked blue and white waves.

**28.** Free-motion machine quilt the waves and the seafoam, making tiny bubble-like stitches in the holes in the seafoam and in the waves. Use a topstitch #90 needle and the same thread you used to create the seafoam. The topstitch needle should leave little holes that resemble bubbles.

Free-motion machine quilt the waves and seafoam in bubble-like stitches.

**29.** Cut the starched palm tree out, moving the fabric not the scissors, giving you more control to create a realistic tree.

**30.** Repeat the process on the sailboat.

**31.** Cut a small wave from the speckled blue and white fabric leftovers to place further out from shore below the sailboat.

**32.** Glue and position the sailboat, palm tree, and wave into place using the photo mat as your guide for placement to make sure all the elements are within the window of the mat. Remove the mat once you have positioned your elements.

**33.** Baste around each of the elements you just positioned with the transparent monofilament thread and a micro-tex #60 needle.

*Tip* A microtex needle tip breaks easily so instead of pushing on the foot pedal, use the hand wheel to start and turn it gently.

**34.** Free-motion machine quilt the palm tree with a matching 30-weight blendable cotton thread using a topstitch #90 needle. Follow the pattern of the fronds on the palm tree.

## Fine Finishing

**1.** On the back side of the photo mat, apply a small bead of Elmer's School Glue down the middle of each side of the mat. Use a small bead of glue otherwise the glue might spread. Try not to touch the front of the mat as the oils from your hands can stain the mat.

**2.** Glue the mat to the quilt.

**3.** Place your matted quilt facedown on a firm surface. Place heavy books on top of the sandwich and leave it to dry overnight.

*Tip* *Always* remove the glass from the frame. Cotton fabrics need to breath and the glass might trap moisture and generate mold.

**4.** Slip your creation in the frame and position the back covering of the frame in place. Remember to add a label or sign the back of the picture frame with your name, the quilt name, the date, and where you live.

# Melanie's Quilt

## Quilt Inspiration and Process

When my dear friend Melanie Duyungan died, I had a very difficult time dealing with her passing, so I made this quilt in her memory. Melanie loved traveling to Italy, especially Tuscany, so I designed a quilt of how I thought a garden in Tuscany might look.

I used a fabric from the Stonehenge Gradations collection by Linda Ludovico by Northcott Fabrics for the grass in this design, shading the left and right edges of the grass using Tsukineko inks. I used an opaque textile paint to paint the brown branches of the shrubs on the left side of the garden wall, and after the paint was dry, I heat-set it. I discovered a flower fabric with the correct scale for the top of the shrubs in my stash, but I didn't like the color. There's always a way to manipulate fabric to make it your own, so to change the color of the flowers, I starched the flower fabric

*Joyce R. Becker, Kent, Washington, 28″ × 28″, 2014*

heavily because it is much easier to color elements on a stiff fabric. Next, I used a purple Fabrico marking pen to change the colors of the flowers from pink to purple and then I heat-set the flower fabric and cut it out.

I wanted the leaves on the shrub with the flowers to appear three-dimensional, so I bonded a darker fabric on the reverse side of the fabric before I cut the leaves out. I also put an overlay of white tulle over the area in the distance to make it look further away, adding to the perspective. I specifically wanted the garden walls to be slightly different colors because the wall on the right of the quilt is in the sun and is lighter in value while the other garden wall is in the shade. I wanted part of the garden wall on the right to have exposed bricks to show its age, so I tried an experiment. (For an explanation of how I accomplished exposing the bricks, see Creating Exposed Bricks on a Wall, page 40.)

To create the pavers in the grass, I sponge painted a gray fabric with white translucent fabric paint and then cut out the pavers individually, decreasing the scale as the path went further in the distance. I colored the bottom edge of each paver with a medium gray wax pastel. The left side of the garden wall includes dense free-motion machine embroidery on the flowers and the foliage, and I used 30-weight cotton matching threads.

# Girly Goat

## Quilt Inspiration and Process

Ever since I saw Laura Heine's cool animal collage quilts, I've wanted to try one of my own. I decided I wanted to put a different slant on my goat, so I placed her in a whimsical landscape rather than a realistic landscape. I traced an enlarged free clip-art drawing of a goat onto Pattern-Ease like Laura uses, but I used my own methods to create Miss Girly Goat.

Laura uses a product called Fabric Fuse (by iCraft) or Steam-A-Seam 2 (by The Warm Company) for fusing her floral motifs on her animal collage quilts but I decided to just skip that step and use my own methods. I traced my enlarged goat onto the Pattern-Ease and then I selected and glued a basic cream fabric for the base of the entire goat. Next, I starched the floral fabrics I selected, cut them out, and glued and positioned them onto the goat individually. Instead of a fusible, I used a Roxanne Glue Stick to adhere my flowers onto the goat. I wanted my *Girly Goat* to have accents of purple, hence the purple horns and ears and so on.

It was fun to try and find wispy flowers for the top edge of Miss Goat, and I laughed myself silly when I found the perfect flower for her beard. I think that the abstract tree and whimsical grass seem to coordinate perfectly with this amusing design. One of my goals with this quilt was to use mostly fabrics in my stash, and I almost succeeded. I did have to purchase the quirky grass fabric and the playful binding fabric, but the rest of the fabrics did come from my stash.

Once this book is published, *Girly Goat* will be gifted to our granddaughter, Matteline Becker, who is a lover of goats. Matteline hopes to one day own a goat or goats, and she enjoys visiting goat rescue facilities and doing goat yoga. I enjoy sending her videos of cute little goats frolicking around.

*Joyce R. Becker, Kent, Washington, 36" × 26", 2016*

From the collection of Matteline Becker

# *Alpine Lake*

## Quiltmaker Profile and Quilt Inspiration

According to Helene, the scene in this quilt depicts Maligne Lake in Jasper National Park, Alberta, Canada. Seeing Helene's *Alpine Lake* quilt for the first time, I found it very appealing, definitely somewhere I would really like to visit in person. It seems like the clouds are ready to swallow up the mountains and that it may be near the end of summer with fall just around the corner. The inner border fabric featuring rocks certainly enhances the design and reinforces the charm of the quilt by coordinating with the rocks on the shoreline. The outer border adds movement without being overbearing.

Regarding techniques in her quilt design, Helene's criteria for her particular methods is based on what the subject is. For example, "For objects that would be static in nature like man-made structures, distant mountains, rocks, or other objects with a hard definition to the edges, I use a turned-edge appliqué technique." For objects that Helene calls "fussy, indistinct, or moving, such as foliage, furry animals, or waterfalls," she uses a raw-edge appliqué technique. In this particular quilt, Helene employed a special technique where she applied liquid adhesive to the very edges of the

*Helene Knott, Oregon City, Oregon, 14" × 19", 2008*

Photo by David Knott

fabric pieces, and she said using this technique resulted in a far more supple and soft quilt than a fused project.

An award-winning quilt artist, Helene's quilts have appeared in books and in magazines. As a special nod to her creativity and expertise, one of her quilts appeared on the cover of *Quilter's Newsletter Magazine*. Helene was nominated for "Teacher of the Year" by *The Professional Quilter* magazine. She is also a fabric designer for Northcott Fabrics and has several fabric lines that were based on her original quilts.

Helene says she is at her happiest when she can just immerse herself into her art.

*Chapter Eleven*

# Fine Finishing Techniques

## Blocking Your Quilt

For those of you who have made primarily traditional quilts in the past, the technique of blocking a quilt may be a new concept. Art quilts or quilts that hang on the wall as art need to hang straight and look like a painting would hanging on the wall. Landscape quilts need to be square, lay flat, and not have any wobbly edges. When you block your landscape quilts, you are basically applying a great deal of moisture to the quilt which in turn actually marries the three layers of the quilt together so when it hangs, it is like one unit instead of a top, batting, and backing. My friend Sonia Grasvik initially taught me how to block my quilts.

I used to block my quilts on a rug on my floor. With age, however, I have changed my methods of blocking. These days, I block my quilts on insulation boards purchased from home improvement stores. These insulation boards are then placed on top of my sewing table so there is no laborious bending over or crawling on the floor. I actually have two insulation boards and depending upon the size of my quilt, I can either use one board by itself or I have the option of taping two of the boards together with blue painter's tape, if necessary. (See the insulation board photo, page 118.)

Blocking is a fairly simple process once you have the supplies. You will need the following: An insulation board, a vinyl flannel-backed tablecloth, a tea towel or a 10″ × 10″ square of muslin to use for pressing, a large bowl of cool water, an iron set on medium to medium-high (*no steam*), and several T-pins.

*Tip* Instead of buying a vinyl flannel-backed tablecloth at the dollar store, invest in a higher-quality tablecloth because sometimes the less-expensive brands melt.

**1.** Place the tablecloth with the flannel side up on top of the insulation board.

**2.** Lay your quilt *facedown* on top of the tablecloth so the back is facing you.

**3.** Secure the edges of the quilt using T-pins. Pin directly into the insulation board. *Do not stretch* your quilt; the T-pins just hold the quilt in place while you block it.

**4.** Dip the pressing cloth into the water until it is very wet and saturated but not dripping.

**5.** Place the cloth over the first corner of the quilt, making sure to include the edges and glide the iron over the surface of the wet cloth until the cloth is dry.

**6.** Continue dampening the pressing cloth and repeat until you have gone over the whole circumference of the quilt. Depending upon the weather, your quilt could be dry by the next day, or if the weather is damp and rainy, it could take several days to dry.

 **I am fortunate to have a ceiling fan over my sewing table, because it speeds up the drying process.**

Blocking a quilt on insulation board

## Squaring

Once your quilt is blocked, it is time to square it. If this is the first time your particular quilt is being squared, that means your quilt probably doesn't have borders. The goal when you square a quilt is to have the measurements be the same from side to side, or up and down, or diagonally. For example, the measurement across your quilt should be the same whether you measure it from across the top, the bottom, or the middle. I normally measure my quilt horizontally in several places to see if the measurements are equal and then I do the same thing for the vertical measurements followed by the diagonal measurements. As you can see, when I measured my quilt *Reflections of Frenchman's Mountain in the Wetlands* (page 74), it measured 18¼" across the quilt horizontally. If I squared it correctly, all the horizontal measurements should be 18¼".

 **Always try to get the top edge of the quilt level first—that's the most important.**

Measurements across the quilt horizontally should be equal, measurements diagonally should be equal, and measurements vertically should be equal.

Squaring a quilt

# Binding or Facing?

## *Binding*

When we discussed whether to add a Border or Not? (page 58), we talked about the other choices we have for our quilts. Sometimes, all a quilt really needs is binding instead of a border. After I finished basting my quilt *The Smoky Mountains* (page 94), I debated on whether to add a border or just binding. I auditioned a fabric that could be used either as a binding or a border by placing the fabric next to my quilt top on my working wall. My final decision was that the border would be distracting using the fabric I selected, but that the same fabric worked perfectly for a binding. My suggestion is that you always audition your possible border and binding fabrics next to your actual quilt top on your working wall to determine which fabric works better or to determine if you think a border isn't really necessary.

A 2½″- or 2¼″-wide strip of fabric works well for binding landscape quilts. Most of you already know how to create a binding, but here is a little tip that might help when you are joining strips together.

> *Tip* **When joining strips to make a diagonal line, I place a dot of glue to hold the 2 strips together instead of pinning, resulting in a more exact seam when I stitch.**

Auditioning fabric for possible borders or binding

Joining binding strips

## Facing

One of the latest trends in art quilts is to finish the quilt with a facing instead of a border or binding. It truly depends on your particular preferences on which direction to go. If your landscape quilt is really thick with several layers of fabric, adding a facing is more difficult when you have to "roll" the facing to the back of the quilt. When I put a facing on my quilt *A Winter's Night* (page 107), it was very successful because there weren't many layers of fabric on the quilt top.

Here is what you need to do if you want to put a facing on your quilt:

**1.** Consider using your backing fabric or a fabric that will blend in with the backing fabric and not be obvious for your facing.

**2.** Measure the sides of the quilt. Cut 2 strips 3″ wide × this length.

**3.** Measure the bottom of your quilt. Cut 1 strip 3″ wide × this length plus ½″.

**4.** Measure the top of your quilt. Cut 1 strip 5½″ wide × this length plus 1″. The top facing will also be your quilt sleeve.

**5.** Turn under ¼″ on one long edge of each strip and press it so that you will have a finished edge on your strips once you turn them to the back of your quilt.

*Tip* To make turning the ¼″ edge easier and more precise, create a ¼″ edge tool to assist you. Place a manila file folder on your rotary mat and cut a ¼″ strip. Place the facing strip on an ironing surface and use the tool to turn the ¼″ seam allowance while you press it with your iron.

**6.** Place the first 3″ fabric strip facedown right sides together on one side of the quilt, pin into place, and stitch a ¼″ seam.

Pin and sew the facing to one side of the quilt top.

**7.** Open the facing and press.

**8.** Next, stitch ⅛″ away from the seam you just stitched on top of the facing strip. This step actually makes it *so* much easier to roll the facing to the back of the quilt.

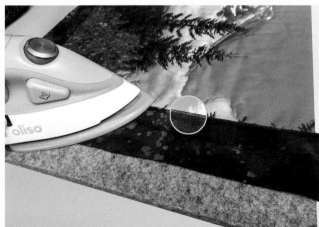

Open and press the facing. Stitch ⅛″ away from the seam you just stitched.

**9.** Roll over the facing strip to the back of the quilt.

**10.** Once the facing is in place, press it again with steam.

**11.** Whipstitch the facing to the back of the quilt with a thread that matches the facing.

**12.** Repeat Steps 6–11 for the other side of the quilt.

**13.** Repeat Steps 6–11 for the bottom edge of the quilt. You will have an extra ¼″ of facing fabric on each side. Tuck the edges in and press and whipstitch the openings closed so that you have a finished edge.

Fold in the edges on the bottom-facing strip.

**14.** Repeat Steps 6–11 for the top edge of the quilt. This facing will also be your hanging sleeve. After you finish stitching the two seams, you should have an extra ½″ so you can tuck the edges in. Tuck the edges in and press. When you whipstitch the facing down, however, do not stitch the openings closed on both sides because they need to be left open so the quilt can be hung.

## The Final Touch

Just when you think you are done with your quilt, here I am to share some other tips that will make it look the best it can when you show to others or exhibit it in public. Now is the time to search for thread tails, lint, unsightly knots, and such, on the front and on the back of your quilt. You can often spot the thread tails when you drape your quilt over the top of a table and turn on a bright light. Use a pair of sharp embroidery scissors to trim any thread trails off. Next, I suggest you use a sticky roller on the front and back of the quilt. Once you do that, your quilt is ready to be admired by others. Be proud of your accomplishment and your creativity. I'm proud of you!

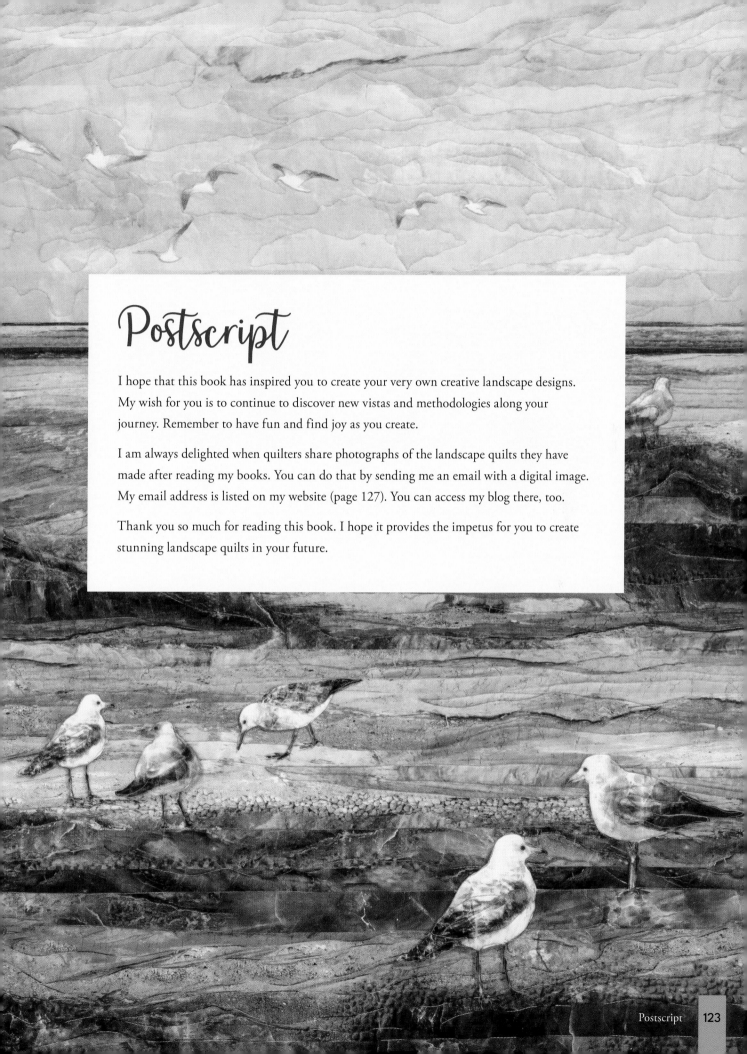

# Postscript

I hope that this book has inspired you to create your very own creative landscape designs. My wish for you is to continue to discover new vistas and methodologies along your journey. Remember to have fun and find joy as you create.

I am always delighted when quilters share photographs of the landscape quilts they have made after reading my books. You can do that by sending me an email with a digital image. My email address is listed on my website (page 127). You can access my blog there, too.

Thank you so much for reading this book. I hope it provides the impetus for you to create stunning landscape quilts in your future.

# Supplies and Resources

*Below are many of the supplies and resources I used in this book. Please check availability of these items first at your local quilt, fabric, craft, and/or art shops. Manufacturer websites are listed for information, but some do not sell directly to consumers.*

## Digital Panels and Commercial Fabrics

**ELIZABETH'S STUDIO**   elizabethsstudio.net
   *Including Winter Companions collection by Abraham Hunter, Landscape Medley collection, and North American Wildlife collection*

**EQUILTER**   equilter.com

**HOFFMAN CALIFORNIA FABRICS**
hoffmancaliforniafabrics.net

**JENNIFER SAMPOU**   jennifersampou.com
   *Including Sky collection precut bundles (also see Robert Kaufman Fabrics for yardage)*

**MICHAEL MILLER FABRICS**   michaelmillerfabrics.com

**MICKEY LAWLER SKYDYES**   skydyes.com

**NORTHCOTT FABRICS**   northcott.com
   *Including Stonehenge Gradations and Stonehenge Gradation Ombré collections by Linda Ludovico and Naturescapes collections by Deborah Edwards*

**P&B TEXTILES**   pbtex.com

**ROBERT KAUFMAN FABRICS**   robertkaufman.com
   *Including Artisan Batiks: Patina Handpaints collection by Lunn Studios and Sky collection by Jennifer Sampou*

**TIMELESS TREASURES FABRICS**   ttfabrics.com

## Prepared-for-Dyeing and Paintable Fabrics

**DHARMA TRADING COMPANY**   dharmatrading.com

## Threads

**INVISAFIL AND COTTON THREADS**
WonderFil Specialty Threads; shopwonderfil.com

**MADEIRA MONOFIL THREAD**   madeira.com

**SULKY BLENDABLES, COTTON+STEEL, AND OTHER COTTON THREADS**   Sulky Threads; sulky.com

## Other Products

*Batting*

**HOBBS THERMORE BATTING**
hobbsbondedfibers.com

*Coloring Tools*

**CARAN D'ACHE NEOCOLOR II WATER SOLUBLE WAX PASTELS**   carandache.com

**LIQUITEX PROFESSIONAL ACRYLIC INK**   liquitex.com

**PRISMACOLOR ARTIST COLORED PENCILS**
prismacolor.com

**TSUKINEKO ALL-PURPOSE INKS**
artisticartifacts.com

**TSUKINEKO FABRICO MARKERS**   imaginecrafts.com

*Color Wheel Tool*

**FOOLPROOF COLOR WHEEL SET**   by Katie Fowler; C&T Publishing; ctpub.com

*Digital Fabric Printing*

**SPOONFLOWER**   spoonflower.com

*Interfacing*

**FAST2FUSE HEAVY INTERFACING**

C&T Publishing; ctpub.com

**PELLON 906F FUSIBLE SHEERWEIGHT**

pellonprojects.com

**PELLON 911FF FUSIBLE FEATHERWEIGHT**

pellonprojects.com

*Repositionable Spray Adhesive*

**ODIF'S 505 TEMPORARY ADHESIVE FOR FABRIC**

odifusa.com

*Scissors*

**KAREN KAY BUCKLEY'S PERFECT SCISSORS—**
**4˝ GREEN AND 6˝ BLUE**   karenkaybuckley.com

*Textile Paints*

**JACQUARD LUMIERE PAINT**   dharmatrading.com

**JACQUARD TEXTILE COLORS**   dharmatrading.com

**PEBEO SETACOLOR FABRIC PAINT**   dharmatrading.com

**PROFAB TRANSPARENT TEXTILE PAINTS**

PRO Chemical & Dye; prochemicalanddye.net

*Tweezers*

**HEIDI PROFFETTY'S PRECISION TWEEZERS**

heidiproffetty.com

**WASH-AWAY STABILIZER:**

**AQUAMESH WASHAWAY**   OESD; oesd.com

## Books

*Fabric Painting with Cindy Walter,* by Cindy Walter
*Laura's Little Book of Collage,* by Laura Heine
Fiberworks Inc.; fiberworks-heine.com

## Photography and Videography

**SIMMONS VIDEO PRODUCTIONS**   *Michael R. Simmons, owner. Photographer of the instructional photos in this book!*

# About the Author

Prize-winning quilter JOYCE R. BECKER focuses her art and writing on landscape quilting. Joyce's books *Quick Little Landscape Quilts*, *Beautifully Embellished Quilts*, and *Luscious Landscapes*, and the DVD *Joyce Becker Teaches You Landscape Quilting*, are all from C&T Publishing. Joyce has made appearances on *Quilting Arts TV* with Susan Brubaker Knapp, *The Quilt Show* with Alex Anderson and Ricky Tims, *Simply Quilts* with Alex Anderson, and *M'Liss's World of Quilts*. Her quilts have been displayed internationally in contests and invitational exhibits and have appeared in books, magazines, and on television.

Joyce's works have been featured in many mainstream quilting magazines, including *Quilting Arts* magazine, and she has written more than twenty feature magazine articles. She has taught on cruises through the Panama Canal, Mexico, Alaska, and the New England coast. Joyce has taught and lectured throughout the United States for guilds and large conferences, including the International Quilt Festival in Houston, Texas; Empty Spools conference in California; and conferences in Canada and New Zealand.

You can find workshops as well as trunk shows and lectures featuring her quilts online. Joyce is also an instructor on the innovative and interactive platform Creative Spark Online Learning (by C&T Publishing); learn about available course options for yourself, your organization, group, or guild.

Photo by Shawn P. Becker

## Visit Joyce online and follow on social media!

WEBSITE: joycerbecker.com

BLOG: joycerbeckerblog.blogspot.com

CREATIVE SPARK: creativespark.ctpub.com

TWITTER: @joycerbecker1

## Also by Joyce R. Becker: